HEALING *the* WOUNDS *of* CHILDHOOD *and* CULTURE

HEALING *the* WOUNDS *of* CHILDHOOD *and* CULTURE

AN ADVENTURE OF A LIFETIME

DON ST JOHN, PH.D.

Archway Publishing books may be ordered through booksellers or by contacting:

Archway Publishing
1663 Liberty Drive
Bloomington, IN 47403
www.archwaypublishing.com
844-669-3957

ISBN: 978-1-6657-2712-9 (sc)
ISBN: 978-1-6657-2710-5 (hc)
ISBN: 978-1-6657-2711-2 (e)

Library of Congress Control Number: 2022913210

Print information available on the last page.

Archway Publishing rev. date: 11/03/2022

This book is dedicated to all of you who intuitively know that "being normal" is so far from who you can truly be. It is dedicated to all of you who know you carry scars of early wounding, who know your childhood was less than perfect, and who may struggle with health, relationship, or well-being issues. It is dedicated to all of you who want to understand fully how you may have been affected and how you can best heal, grow, and thrive.

I dedicate it as well to all the psychotherapists and counselors who want to understand where the body fits into healing and growth and to all the "body people"—from physicians to somatic therapists, acupuncturists, and bodyworkers—who want to understand how upbringing and relationships influence the bodies they work with.

Acclaim for *Healing the Wounds of Childhood and Culture*

This authoritative and comprehensive exploration of healing and wellness is also a riveting page-turner full of practical advice and personal stories, including from the author's own traumatic childhood. It offers a remarkable and uncommon integration of brain science, mainstream psychology, and cutting-edge ideas and practices. Effective, hopeful, and profound, this is a gem.

Rick Hanson, PhD, author of *Buddha's Brain* and *Hardwiring Happiness: The New Brain Science of Contentment, Calm, and Confidence*

Don St. John's book is a huge accomplishment, a miraculous personal journey intertwined with the miraculous evolution of many disciplines seeking to understand mind and human heart to help people heal. Despite the pervasiveness of trauma amply manifested in the author's own beginnings, his theme is that love is ever abundant—if we learn how to receive it and how to take it in so that we can thrive. Read this book to learn about the evolution of science and the field of psychotherapy. Read this book to learn about one man's journey from trauma to lovability. And read this book to get some wonderful, sage, truly tried-and-true advice about how you too can apply these lessons to make your journey sweeter and richer.

Dr. Diana Fosha, developer of AEDP and author of *The Healing Power of Affect* and *The Healing Power of Emotion: Affective Neuroscience, Development and Clinical Practice,* edited with Daniel Siegel and Marion Solomon

We are very pleased to recommend Don's book to all of you. *Healing the Wounds of Childhood and Culture* is really two different offerings. First of all, it is a very personal anecdotal document that lays out the raw wounds of his life and how he dealt with them. In opening his personal process to us, he also has given to his readers a clear and intimate view of a wide range of therapeutic disciplines. Thirdly he is able to tie it all together with a combination of wisdom, clarity, and always a sense of presence in relationship to the material and to the reader. The wounds of our life are made to be healed by our efforts rather than being drowned in the sense of victimhood that so easily can run our life. Don's writing is a gift to those of us who do our best to travel the path of consciousness and to those of us who are looking for how to begin the journey.

Hal Stone, PhD, and Sidra Stone, PhD, authors of *Embracing Our Selves: The Voice Dialogue Manual; Embracing Each Other: How to Make All Your Relationships Work for You; Embracing the Inner Critic: Turning Self Criticism into a Creative Asset; The Shadow King: The Invisible Force That Holds Women Back;* and *Partnering: A New Kind of Relationship*

In this book, Don St. John draws on his personal experience to develop a model of integration that is both simple and profoundly effective. He begins by looking at the values that are really important to our development as people. He illustrates his points by describing experiences from his personal and his professional development with the sort of sensitivity that can result from deep wounding. After a thorough tour of all the physiological as well as the psychological elements of a healthy life, he delivers an intelligent and coherent pathway to integrate all the various aspects of our lives and to literally incorporate the lessons from both our positive and our "negative" experiences. It is a pathway in that it includes for each aspect some practical steps to integrate that aspect. An inspired and inspiring work of synthesis, I think it is brilliant!

Joseph Heller, author of *Bodywise* and founder of Hellerwork Structural Integration.

Contents

Acknowledgments

This book would never have been written without the love and support of my wife, partner, and dearest friend, Diane. I don't mean that just in the sense of the enormous generosity of time and energy that she has contributed. Indeed, she has tirelessly read each version of the manuscript and has been among my sharpest critics—editing, suggesting, and urging for more clarity. Of course, this in itself has been hugely helpful. More importantly, however, I have been able to write this book because she is the person who, along with me, forged something neither one of us knew in the past: a strong, enduring, intimate marriage that seems to improve with every passing year. Without this, I would not have the ground, the moral standing, to speak of a thriving life.

I want to thank our very dear friend Elizabeth Anne Sutcliffe for her courageous feedback and support. My first edition editor, Sarah Aschenbach, did a great job.

Joseph Heller has been both mentor and friend for over forty years. Many years ago, he predicted that I would write this type of book. I owe a great deal to Emilie Conrad and Susan Harper, mentors who taught me something about what it means to be alive in this body.

Thank you to my oldest and dear friends Jerry and Nancy Noloboff, who throughout this writing expressed their love and support.

And to my brother, Rocky. I have loved you since the day you were born.

And to Debbie, Matt, Elias, and Ruth, I thank you from the depths of my heart for being such a great family.

Introduction to Part 1

Embarking on a healing journey is the surest way to a rewarding, adventurous, meaningful, vibrant life. It is the most certain way to grow self-knowledge and to discover new aspects of ourselves. We can live life with a growing sense of agency, a sense of "I'm the one in charge of my life," and simultaneously a growing sense of alignment with a higher order—whether religious, spiritual, or secular—a sense of something supportive beyond the limits of our body-mind. When committed to this journey, higher energies will present themselves, even if only in the form of improbable coincidences or even a sequence of improbable events. My surviving a serious heart attack without any medical treatment for three months was one of those for me. But I'm getting well ahead of myself here. Among the joys that can be found along this path is sustained emotional and sexual intimacy, the likes of which one may have never even imagined. In my seventy-ninth year, I can say with utter confidence that my voyage continues, and a remarkable journey it is.

Healing means to become whole; to become whole does not mean to reach a static state of "now I'm whole." It can be an ever-growing "felt-sense" of wholeness. It does not mean only a relief of symptoms. Healing is an ongoing process of identifying, claiming, integrating, refining, letting go, and developing aspects of ourselves. It hugely involves letting go—of bad habits, addictions, vices, ways of perceiving, and ways of being in the world that are limiting or have negative consequences. It's a process of discovery, even learning we do not have to age in the same way our parents and grandparents did. What I am suggesting is an adventure in every sense of the word, replete with surprises, with sublime moments, with challenges, with many bonding experiences, with discomforts, with plateaus, with periods of rests and renewal, and most importantly, with emotional, spiritual, somatic, and relational growth.

Perhaps most importantly, becoming whole means recognizing that we are the authors of our own lives. This is not always an easy concept to grasp or accept. Things happen to us; we are born into a family whose genetics and conditions have profound influences over our lives and over the choices we make. Nevertheless, from the very beginning of our lives, and however subconscious it may be, we are interpreting and making meaning of the events that occur.

This is the single most powerful perspective we can assume. It is the opposite of feeling and believing oneself to be a victim. Before wondering if I live in the world of Pollyanna, let me tell you I received some serious challenges, from conception through adolescence. Nearly dying at birth and being on the receiving end of my mother's slaps across the face starting at eleven months old, I know what trauma feels like. I went numb. My only recourse was to live solely in my head. As a young adult, emotional intimacy was something I only read about. There were other symptoms as well. So, Pollyanna has never been one of my characteristics. I know how rough life can be.

One morning in my twentieth year as an airman in the US Air Force, I woke up in the back seat of my car, bleeding in my throat. I had been extremely drunk the night before and was hollering and carrying on. In that moment, I made a fateful choice. "I need help!" Searching through the Yellow Pages, I found a psychiatrist who could see me on a Saturday. It was fifty-eight years ago. Little did I know I was on the threshold of a completely new life.

Decades later, I live in a world that often feels enchanting, a world with a sense that there is enough. There is enough love, enough care, enough of what I need. I live with immense gratitude for all I have received along the way, spiritually, materially, emotionally, and relationally. At first, I was simply going to a psychiatrist to relieve symptoms. At some point, it all changed. Symptom relief is barely the beginning. There is so much more to discover, and not just in psychotherapy.

As we begin to comprehend what is possible for us as human beings, we have a choice to go for it or not. There is so much suffering in our world. So many are desperately lonely; so many suffer from relationship distress, chronic illness, addictions, meaninglessness, or just a sense of living a vacuous life. Money and success render no one immune from these afflictions. In fact, they can intensify the pain since we have been led to believe money and success represent the pinnacle of achievement and happiness.

Our culture is wounded. If we add up the percentage of Americans who will receive a cancer diagnosis before reaching a ripe old age, the percentage of us who are considered obese, the percentage who will have diabetes or heart disease, the percentage who live on the margins of poverty, the numbers dying from deaths of despair such as suicides or opioid overdoses, what other conclusion can we draw? Our culture is hurting *badly*. So many metrics point to this conclusion.

In the US, polarization has reached levels not seen in decades. It's as if we are two different and antagonistic countries. And it goes on and on. We have had horrible schisms in the US before. The Civil War was the epitome. Yet we have so much more in common than we believe. Underlying all schisms is a fundamental error in our comprehension of what it means to be a human being. We are here to learn to embrace polarities and to evolve compassion and comprehension. We are here to recognize how much of what we need is already available, freely given. We are here to grow in every way, including growing virtues.

In the *New York Times* (September 10, 2020), Pulitzer Prize-winning columnist Nicholas Kristof quotes a recent study showing that the US ranks twenty-eighth in the well-being of its citizens. The US ranks number one in the world in quality of universities, but number ninety-one in access to quality education. The US leads the world in medical technology, yet we are number ninety-seven in access to quality health care.

The materialistic model of what it means to be a human is woefully insufficient. Those who have really good marriages, families, and material success are the fortunate. Yet to believe this is all life has to offer is simply not true. We are in dire need of a new model of what it means to be a human being! A model that doesn't separate every important aspect of human existence, a model that recognizes that physical health, somatic awareness, emotional well-being, relational satisfaction, and spiritual development must be viewed as a whole.

Providing a view of what else life has to offer is the purpose of this book. What our culture offers us is limited, constricted, suffocating, and wounding. I say this not merely as an indictment of our culture but as an invitation to jump in, come aboard, and engage the adventure that has no limits.

I was fortunate to have received so much emotional and physical abuse in my early life. Why would I make such a statement? Because my choices were stark: live a life of awful self-esteem, addictions, relationship dysfunction, chronic illness, and a certain early death or embark on this journey. I say fortunate because were it not for the extent of my early suffering, I may not have taken the leap. I may have remained in the comfort of what I had been shown to be the arena of my life. What a loss that would have been—a loss of both the benefits accrued and the very process itself. Truly an adventure!

What I am proposing is that this journey is for all of us. That the foundation of our lives, our comprehension, our assumptions, and our beliefs have all contributed to a field of limitation in which so many are seriously wounded, and most don't know what is available. We would all benefit enormously in so many ways by embarking on the journey toward wholeness.

I can't promise it will be the same for you. I simply cannot think of anything that has the potential to offer more. In chapter 1, I will invite you to forget anything about being normal. Normal is a statistical concept; it should not be what we are seeking. I will also present a model, a way of understanding health—physical health, emotional well-being, relationship satisfaction, and spiritual development—a model that provides a direction and an ideal.

In chapter 2, I describe how we have been wounded. The primary dimensions of our being that have been wounded are authorship—or the sense of responsibility for our lives—identity, and connections. Chapter 3 describes familial and cultural wounds. In chapter 4, we examine how our core beliefs, usually below the threshold of consciousness, together with our sense of who we are shapes our very reality. In this sense, we "create our own reality."

In chapter 5, we'll see how our brains require emotional intimacy for its optimal development. Ideally this occurs throughout our infancy and childhood. Fortunately, because of the brain's plasticity, emotional intimacy will support growth at any age. Chapters 6 and 7 will deal with stress and the effects of stress on our health.

Stress is one of those ambiguous terms, and we will look at some of the mechanisms of stress and the ways our health is affected by stress. Our autonomic nervous system plays an important role in stress, health, and trauma. In the past couple of decades, a new model of the workings of the ANS has been developed by neuropsychologist Stephen Porges. In chapter 8, we will examine this model. Very much related to our autonomic nervous system is our heart. We discuss our heart in chapter 9, not as a mechanical pump but as a partner of our brain and a center of consciousness. We conclude part 1 of this book with a look at the tissues of our body. The quality of our muscle and connective tissues is rarely considered in any conversation of health and well-being. We will see in chapter 10 why our tissue quality is important.

In part 2 of this book, we will look at four dimensions of being, which I believe must be considered to appreciate the full process of moving toward wholeness. They are the somatic,* the psychological, the relational, and the spiritual. If you're interested in personal growth, healing, or spiritual evolution, I think you'll find this book a helpful companion.

* I use the term *somatic* to refer not only to the body but more accurately to the experience of one's body from the inside. This concept will be elaborated in various sections of this book and especially in chapter 11.

1

A New Model of Health and Well-Being

"Is that normal, Dr. Don?" How many times have I heard that question? My client has just finished expressing a list of concerns. Lurking and haunting in the background is the question of normality. We want to be normal. Have you ever worried about whether you are "normal"? Somewhere in the recesses of your mind, do you harbor doubts about whether you are like most other people? If you're struggling with intimacy challenges, if you experience frequent anxiety or depression, if you have mood swings, or if you have an addiction—to alcohol, drugs, sex, or chocolate—do you believe you are part of a small percentage of the population with a disorder and wish to somehow be normal? Probably most of us have questioned our normality at one point or another. Yet given the data, statistically normal should not be our highest aim in life. We are unique beings, and crafting, refining, and shining our uniqueness is a much more rewarding pursuit.

A much more useful way to commence upon this journey is to recognize we are all in the same boat! Sure, some of us may be sitting toward the front and some of us in the back, but it is the same boat. We all are far from optimal, and we can all improve along many dimensions that enrich our lives beyond what most of us believe to be possible. This is a much more useful, compassionate, and healthy way to think about our personal journey.

In time, a new model of what it means to be healthy both physically and emotionally will prevail. The model I envision will view relationship health, emotional health, physical health, and spiritual development as interrelated. An important step on this path is to let go of the concept of normality. Let's no longer ask if we are normal; let's ask what is possible. Can I feel stronger at seventy-eight than I did at forty-seven? Can I feel more "in" my body, enjoy a fuller sense of self, explore more refined spiritual energies, or enjoy new aspects of my sexuality? The answer is a resounding yes. It does take commitment, willingness, perseverance, and comprehension—as does traversing any breathtakingly beautiful terrain while on a great adventure.

In order for what I am suggesting to make sense, we need to see how our culture implicitly employs a model that is in itself part of the problem rather than part of the solution. We assume normality is the ideal then define "normality" in terms of the absence of symptoms. This logic is what keeps many, if not most, people from even considering engaging disciplines and practices that can dramatically further their development over a lifetime. Given how everything is compartmentalized, specialized, and mechanized, we fail to see critical relationships among various aspects of our lives. For example, we tend not to realize how the quality of our intimate relationships and lovemaking can affect our physical health. Or how our deep beliefs affect our relationships and well-being. Where should we look to find a model that can give us an ideal toward which to strive? As bizarre as this may initially sound, I believe this model we see is water. Yes, water!

I find it bizarre that 99 percent of all molecules in the human body are water molecules (some 60 to 70 percent by volume), yet there is just a modicum of scientific investigation of water. It may just be that water itself provides answers to questions concerning health, fitness, intimate relationships, and spiritual comprehension. It is because we are primarily water that we have such an amazing capacity to change. Of course, most of us don't feel very fluid. This is a cultural wound. When has anyone even heard that being "fluid" is a valuable thing? Yet given the percentage of our biology that is in fact fluid, we might say being in touch with our fluidity is being in touch with reality.

As I began writing this book, I still lacked a unifying concept. All the pieces were there; I knew the importance of healthy supporting beliefs, of good relational skills, and of a good physical structure. I knew that although our current model of health and fitness (exercise, diet, and stress management) represented a leap forward from the fifties and sixties, still they weren't quite sufficient. I also knew we couldn't separate body, mind, and relationships. A holistic understanding was clearly necessary and clearly closer to the truth. Yet I didn't have a single concept that put the whole picture together. I had all the ingredients to make a cake; I just didn't know what the cake was. I was yet to realize that water provides an integrative model of life.

Then I came upon the work of Dr. Mae-Wan Ho. She has written two books. Her first, *The Rainbow and the Worm: The Physics of Organisms,*[1] sent shivers coursing down my spine. It provides ample evidence for the idea that consciousness and our experiences of life do not reside only in the brain. Rather, they reside throughout our entire organism. Dr. Ho is looking at the biology of an organism through the lenses of quantum physics and is arriving at some fascinating conclusions. It is well beyond the scope of this book to attempt an elaborate explanation of her visionary work. I will simply share what I have derived from reading it. The extrapolations of her thoughts to the structure of the body, the personality, and our intimate relationships are mine.

The prevailing medical/psychological paradigm essentially equates the mind with the brain and views the rest of the body as its servant. This fundamental premise informs our culture's model of health, well-being, fitness, and yes, even relationships. As the implications of quantum physics for cell biology becomes part of the general scientific and medical narrative, I believe we will become much better equipped to take good care of ourselves and to heal the wounds that limit our potential. Specifically, I believe we will come to understand that physical fitness, emotional health, relational capacities, and spiritual evolution are all part of a whole and must be thought of as a whole. For example, a fit person is not one who can simply run ten miles or has abs of steel. A fit person is one whose tissues are also *responsive, receptive, adaptive, versatile, fluid,* and *vibrant.* This presents a very different picture of fitness. More accurately, what we are pursuing in this model is coherence or integration.

The Rainbow and the Worm describes the living organism as coherent, which Dr. Ho defines as "a state in which both individual freedom and global cohesion are maximized." She uses a jazz band as a metaphor to illustrate her point. Each musician does his or her own thing and in perfect harmony with the whole band. The quality of the music is determined by how well the players perform, the vitality, heart, and soul with which they play their own instrument, *and* how well they play in unison with every other member of the band, which shows how sensitive and responsive they are to their fellow musicians. This is a good example of individual or local freedom *and* global cohesion.

Dr. Ho's books give a rigorously scientific definition of coherence in mathematical terms. However, for our purposes, the metaphor of the jazz band is sufficient and indeed apt. All living organisms, from the amoeba to the human being, are ideally coherent. "They are thick with coherent activities on every scale, from the macroscopic down to the molecular and below."[2] We will return to this concept of maximum individuality and maximum cohesiveness or closeness again and again. As you will see, it's intuitively obvious that it is an ideal in many areas of our lives, from our own physical structures to our intimate relationships.

In her second book, *Living Rainbow H2O,*[3] she presents extensive evidence that it is the very fact that we are composed mostly of water that accounts for our capacity to change and adapt. Mae-Wan Ho applies quantum physics and electrodynamics field theory to the biochemistry of water, concluding that quantum coherence is possible because of the large percentage of water that constitutes an organism.

> *Quantum jazz is the music of the organism dancing life into being. It is played out by the whole organism, in every nerve and sinew, every muscle, every single cell, molecule, atom, and elementary particle ...*
>
> *Intercommunication is the key to quantum jazz. It is done to such sublime perfection that each molecule is effectively intercommunicating with every other, so each is as much in control as it is sensitive and responsive. And intercommunication is predominantly electronic and electromagnetic, thanks to liquid crystalline water.*[4]

What a different picture from the conventional notion that the nervous system is the primary communication system in the body. What is liquid crystalline water? We've all been taught that water has three phases: liquid, solid, and vapor. Enter the work of Dr. Gerald Pollack, who has devoted a good portion of his long career as a bioengineering scientist to studying a fourth phase of water. His book *The Fourth Phase of Water* describes numerous experiments demonstrating the existence and properties of this fourth phase, which he calls the exclusionary zone or EZ zone.[5] Essentially, this is a semiliquid phase of water, the viscosity of which is akin to a raw egg white or to honey. This is liquid crystalline water.

Most of the water in the human body is in this fourth phase. One of the characteristics of this phase is it stores energy. Light creates the processes that store this energy. Water stores energy and water gets energy from light. "The sun's electromagnetic energy builds potential energy in water. Photons recharge the EZ by building order and separating charge. They do this by splitting water molecules, ordering the EZ, and thereby setting up one charge polarity in the ordered zone and the opposite polarity in the bulk water zone beyond."[6]

The EZ is negatively charged, as is the earth. We are receiving negative charge from the earth, and the light of the sun energizes the water in our body. This is why it feels so good to walk barefoot on the earth while the sun shines brilliantly upon us. As the fluids of our body become more vital and energized, the more coherent we become.

The fluid system is the fundamental system of communication. (Emilie Conrad)

The implications of Mae-Wan Ho's and Gerald Pollack's works are staggering. One implication is this: consciousness is, at a minimum, one with the whole organism. The brain is a critical organ of consciousness. But listen to what Dr. Ho says after she has considered the implications of quantum physics for biological organisms.

> *Whenever people speak of consciousness, they usually locate it in the brain where ideas and intentions are supposed to flow, and which through the nervous system, is supposed to control the entire body. I have always found that odd, for like all Chinese people, I was brought up on the idea that thoughts emanate from the heart. I have come to the conclusion that a more accurate account is that consciousness is delocalized throughout the liquid crystalline continuum of the body (including the brain), rather than just being localized to our brain or to our heart. By consciousness, I include, at the*

minimum, the faculties of sentience (responsiveness), intercommunication, as well as memory.[7]

What might it mean to accept that consciousness is located throughout the liquid crystalline continuum of the whole body? What might that mean for physical education and physical fitness? What might it mean for health and self-care? Certainly, from the science of Mae Wan-Ho and Gerald Pollack, we can intuitively sense the absolute correctness of considering the organism as a whole. The territory of our healing adventure is far greater than just our minds.

Another phenomenal implication of the fact that our body is comprised mostly of water is that we are able to make profound changes and develop strong resilience. Water is famous for its capacity to adapt. Neuroscientists now tell us that the human brain has the capacity to change and improve throughout the life span, using words like *neuroplasticity, neurogenesis,* and *synaptogenesis.* This is certainly true, but we cannot stop with the brain. The science in Dr. Ho's books is clear. The whole organism is involved because the organism is mostly water, which circulates throughout the body. What has more adaptive capacity than water? Water is fluid, yet what power it has! And so, too, is our nature—fluid and powerful.

Take a drink. Inside you the water whispers: "And now you are a million years old." (Mary Oliver)

The old model of consciousness as an epiphenomenon of the brain, all located in our heads, is beginning to fade. In his brilliant work *Mind: A Journey to the Heart of Being Human,*[8] psychiatrist Daniel Siegel goes even further than Dr. Ho in his comprehension of where consciousness is located. Whereas Dr. Ho describes consciousness in terms of the whole organism, Dr. Siegel defines it in terms of the whole organism *and* its connections. What constitutes "my mind" is not only a function of my entire body but also the connections I am experiencing at any given moment. He describes the organization and flow of energy and information within and between. The model he uses to assess the quality of that organization is integration. Integration is defined as differentiation *and* linkage. This concept of integration is very much like Dr. Ho's coherence, which is why I am using them interchangeably.

Siegel employs the concept of integration to define health. He uses the metaphor of the flow of a river. Flow with healthy banks is health; it's a state of integration. Two things can interfere with the integrated flow of the river. On one side is chaos. On the other is rigidity. Going through *The Diagnostic and Statistical Manual*, the bible of mental disorders, he asserted that all diagnoses could be seen as either excessive chaos or excessive rigidity. In other words, diagnoses are descriptions of where and how integration is compromised.

In Dan Siegel's thinking, the very concept of "me" should be replaced by the concept "Mwe." In other words, he is saying that the fundamental reality isn't the separate, individual self. It is relationship. What I consider my mind, and what I have been taught to localize in the brain, is actually—if Siegel's hypothesis is borne out—located within my entire brain and body and in the flow of energy and information between us.

There is an emerging new story of what it means to be a human being. Perhaps no one articulates how the old story came to be and what is now emerging quite like Charles Eisenstein. In his monumental work *The Ascent of Humanity,*[9] Eisenstein describes what he terms the "story of separation." In great detail he describes the inevitable march of humanity toward greater separation, from the environment, the earth, the water, the sun, the moon, and each other. The choices made along the way, he says, were inevitable, the result culminating in a philosophy that human beings are separate creatures whose lot in life is to control and manipulate the objective world that exists separate from us. What we need is a new story of who we are. Looking at the great challenges of our time—climate change, environmental pollution, divisiveness, immigration, poverty, education, and more—can only be solved if we address the deepest cause: the story we tell that we are separate, discreet beings with no inherent connection to one another or to the environment in which we live.

The study of water may be what provides more understanding of what it means to be a human being. In a review of Gerald Pollack's, *The Fourth Stage of Water*, Eisenstein asserts that Pollack's book may be part of a revolution in scientific thinking. Listen to his words. "It contributes to a much larger paradigm shift that is proceeding across all the sciences, and indeed to the defining mythology of our civilization." In science alone, the implications of his findings, if verified, are profound. Beyond that, they erode the story that we live in a dead universe of generic substances, that we, the sole intelligence of that universe, are therefore its rightful lords and masters. Pollack is part of the evolution of science toward a more shamanic worldview that understands that all things possess some kind of "beingness."

The work of Mae-Wan Ho, Gerald Pollack, Dan Siegel, and Charles Eisenstein move us toward a new story, not of separation but of connection. Coherence—or integration—leads us to a journey of healing: a journey toward wholeness. They give us a road map to follow. Whether we are looking at our body and being, our intimate relationships, or our connection to nature, integration is the direction we need to go. It is an adventure of unlimited dimensionality, challenge, and reward. It is a lifetime journey.

We can bounce back or recover from trauma and abuse, loss and disappointments, and defeats and frustrations. We can learn to give and receive love, grow the courage and strength to direct the course of our life, learn to be gentle and receptive, and connect deeply with others while taking good care of ourselves. We can even grow the capacity to feel nourished simply by being alive and awake in our body. To become more coherent means to become more present and to recognize that we are connected to all living things; therefore, any action that harms other people renders us less coherent.

As we become more coherent, we become more appreciative of the web of life—and of our freedom within it, coupled with a deep sense of belonging to and being a part of all life. As we become more coherent, I believe, we recognize the folly of rigid polarities. We gradually come to own what we have previously disowned and learn to develop a more compassionate, loving, and peaceful heart. What could be more important?

Notes

1. Ho, Mae-Wan, *The Rainbow and the Worm: The Physics of Organisms,* World Scientific Publishing, 1998.
2. Ho, Mae-Wan, *Living Rainbow H2O,* World Scientific Publishing, p. 4, 2012.
3. Ho, Mae-Wan, *Living Rainbow H2O,* World Scientific Publishing, 2012.
4. *Ibid*, pp. 4–5.
5. Pollack, Gerald, *The Fourth Phase of Water,* Ebner and Sons Publishers, pp. 332–333, 2013.
6. Pollack, p. 335.
7. Ho, Mae-Wan, *The Rainbow and the Worm: The Physics of Organisms,* World Scientific Publishing, p. 185, 1998.
8. Siegel, Daniel J., Mind: *A Journey to the Heart of Being Human,* W.W. Norton and Company, 2017.
9. Eisenstein, Charles, *The Ascent of Humanity: Civilization and the Human Sense of Self,* North Atlantic Books, 2013.

2

We've All Been Wounded

How does so much wounding come about? The most general answer is the atmosphere into which we are born. By atmosphere, I am referring to the philosophical, spiritual, and environmental climate of the era in which we are born and raised. Our cultural environment implicitly informs us of what's expected, what's allowed or not allowed, what we should aim for, and why we are even on the earth.

For example, what it means to be a man in the twenty-first century is different from what it meant to be a man in the ninth century. Our cultural understanding provides the parameters of our being, and to the degree this comprehension limits our spiritual, psychological, somatic, or relational growth, it is wounding. It creates a gaping hole in who we take ourselves to be.

Many of us were reared in the Judeo-Christian heritage. I was raised in the Catholic Church, where I was taught that if I died with a mortal sin on my soul, I would burn in hell for all eternity. Mortal sins included giving oneself sexual pleasure, missing Mass on Sundays, and disobeying one's parents. Burn for eternity. What a devastating concept. If I died with venial sins on my soul, then a time of burning in purgatory would be required before I could enter the gates of paradise. Every six-year-old child knows what it feels like to put his finger too close to a flame. It is terrifying to imagine contemplating one's whole body immersed forever in flames. That kind of nonsense should be outlawed. Yet fire and damnation have been part of our Christian heritage for centuries.

Are you a "God-fearing" man? "Behave or you could be eternally damned" is a belief still held by many millions. A God who is exacting, demanding, or frightening leaves his children with a pervasive sense of inadequacy and fear. This deep belief that I can be never good enough is pervasive. Many of my patients over the years have struggled to cultivate the strength to not let others push them around because they conflated strength or directness with cruelty and being unkind. Their religion taught them to always be nice, compliant, and agreeable. The "thou shalt, and thou shalt nots" are notorious for the many hang-ups they have wrought upon their believers. Usually, there is a kernel of wisdom in the prescriptions and injunctions, but they can be so easily corrupted by overzealous and conflicted ministers of the faith.

Further, many conventional churches focus merely on ethics and morals without realizing that in a spiritual process, ethics and morals are preparatory to opening to the mysteries and higher teachings found in every religion. While ethics and morals are important, what true spirituality offers is some level of illumination, meaning—at a minimum—the recognition of our authorship of our lives, an expanded sense of identity, and a profound sense of connectedness to nature and to each other. This is the function of a true spiritual path. To not know that life offers this possibility contributes to the stultifying of everyday life.

Then there is the secular contribution to the "atmosphere" of our lives. I appreciate the work of science and the phenomenal results that science has brought to our material lives. Yet, I find it utterly distressing that a major political party and millions of its adherents dismiss or denigrate science. I find it distressing, but I don't find it completely baffling. Why? Because I believe science must take some responsibility for a portion of the antipathy it is receiving. The belief, held by many, that science is the only way to truly know, and the belief that what can't be measured either doesn't exist or isn't worth studying, is called "scientism" or science as religion.[1]

These unquestioned assumptions help define who we are, and the definition that emerges is in itself wounding. It elevates the rational mind to be the "supreme knower," while all of what's most important to human existence, such as purpose, commitment, wisdom, intuition, and love, live on the periphery of science. The extraordinary manifestations of human existence—miracles, psychic phenomena, mystical experiences, astrology, numerology, etc.—are simply not taken seriously.

This is part of a much larger dynamic of how the religion of science can narrow the frontiers of our lives. It is the pernicious and widely held belief that if science has not stamped its *imprimatur*—its stamp of approval--on a particular activity, discipline, or process, it is not deemed worthy of our consideration.

So far, we have identified two major forces that, if not questioned and examined, can limit our potential: religion that doesn't quite comprehend the purpose of religion and science that eschews religion without acknowledging it, too, is a major religion.

Next, let's look at the lenses through which the mental health profession sees the world. Mental health approaches contribute to the atmosphere that fails to view the healing journey as the adventure it really is. "Am I normal?" is a question I hear over and over in countless forms. Here's the problem: as long as we accept the absence of symptoms as normal and the goal we should strive toward, we are without the comprehension necessary to pursue what's possible, our own beautiful uniqueness. More and more psychotherapy has come under the sway of the medical model and the ubiquitous insurance industry. It's about curing symptoms and submitting codes to the insurance company. The medical model has prevailed. Lost is probing the depths of our unconscious and uncovering parts of ourselves heretofore disowned.

We need guides, elders, and wisdom holders for this journey I am describing.

There is one more general factor to mention that affects our health and well-being: our physical environment. The quality of our water, the quality of the air we breathe, the soil in which we grow our food, and the manner in which we feed and house our livestock all have an impact on the quality of our lives. Clean air, healthy food, and pure water make a difference. They are important to our health and well-being.

Now let's look at personal factors that contribute to the wounds of our lives.

Trauma

Trauma has become the buzzword of mental health. Many patients over the years have told me that they experienced very little "trauma" in childhood. Initially, they say they had a normal childhood. Then, within the next fifteen minutes, they tell me their mom was depressed for two years after their birth or their father was an alcoholic who often came home enraged. Many tell me their parents never openly expressed affection to them or to each other and feelings didn't exist in their homes. But there was "no trauma." Theirs was a "normal childhood."

Further, the word *trauma* itself is used in so many different ways that nonprofessionals can be easily confused. For example, the literature on trauma speaks of the following concepts: big-T trauma, little-t trauma, relational trauma, developmental trauma, shock trauma, and probably others. This does not make it easy for the laymen to answer the question "Was I traumatized in my youth?"

Further, the yes/no model of trauma keeps us stuck in a way that suggests treatment is only for those individuals who "have the disease." Some symptoms of trauma are found in many of us who would not be classified with PTSD. For example, many human beings are disconnected to some degree from their emotions, from the felt-sense of their bodies, or from parts of themselves. Many individuals who would not be classified with PTSD are hypervigilant, tense, anxious, or hyperaroused (meaning they are quick to flare). To suggest that only those with PTSD should receive treatments belies the fact that most of us would benefit enormously by utilizing the resources available for lessening the effects of trauma.

Obviously, if a person has been sexually, physically, or emotionally abused, there will, most likely, be deep wounds to heal. But what about, for example, an individual whose mother was depressed for the first two years of her life? Most likely this person would not consider herself traumatized. In her memory, her mother was a caring and kind person. Yet to have a depressed mom for the first two years of one's life can be torturous to an infant craving presence and attunement. There are many such examples.

Over decades I've worked with many individuals who were perplexed by relationship, self-esteem, and other emotional challenges. They were reared in "normal" homes and cared for by two "normal" parents. "What's wrong with me?" is the most typical outcome of this type of situation. Important needs have not been met, but there is no way for a child to know and articulate this. He experiences it as his deficiency. This type of situation is not rare at all.

A positive environment is important to a child's growing sense of well-being. Recently a patient told me that, unlike her partner, she had had a good childhood. Except—oh, by the way, her parents divorced when she was three, and her mother then married her father's best friend. They divorced two years later. Soon after this divorce, her mother remarried her father. Usually, a couple experiences at least two or three years of strife before a divorce. My patient was breathing in and absorbing through her pores the emotional vibrations of the household beginning in infancy, and those vibes were not those of happy people.

Children feel the emotional tones of their homes. They feel pain when their parents don't really love each other, especially if there is hostility and resentment. When the hostility, resentment, or pain of our parents is denied and there is a pretense of "all is well," the tension of the parents will be passed on to their children. Children are very sensitive to the vibrations in a home. It's folly to believe that if we don't tell them in words, they'll be oblivious to the strife, pain, or rancor that permeates the airwaves.

Of course, transparency doesn't mean confessing every detail; it means finding a way to help children make sense of what they are feeling. If not, they will learn to distrust their own feelings, distrust you, or some combination of both. How many of us had parents who were capable of helping us make sense of what we were feeling? How many of us as adults feel very competent in making sense of our feelings? This is a skill we can grow as we travel the path I am proposing.

If parents are preoccupied, chronically worried, having an affair, abusing drugs or alcohol, or implicitly delivering double messages to their children, the hurt goes deep. Here are examples of a double message. "I want you to be independent, as long as you do it my way." "I want you to come closer. But if you come close, I'll get scared and back away." Sound familiar? Can you think of a double message that you received throughout your childhood?

Here are two other wounding situations that can be difficult to discern. The first is when a parent very early on begins to treat the child as if the child is responsible for the parent's well-being or security. It is as if the parent's inner child is terribly insecure and begins to look to the child's inner parent to provide security. In this situation, the child feels pressure to grow up quickly and as an adult has a challenge connecting with the child part of himself. Of course, underneath, as therapy progresses, a good deal of grief and anger is uncovered. It is an enormous loss to have to relinquish one's childhood to become a caretaker.

Another often hard to discern but virulent situation is when one or both parents have strong narcissistic issues. Some years ago, I had a client, Fiona, who came to me because of relationship and self-esteem issues. She couldn't recall a time when her mother showed any genuine interest in her. Whatever she would bring to Mom would be turned around and framed as what it meant for Mom. It was Fiona's job to figure out what Mom needed and provide it.

The second part of her dilemma was that she could never succeed. Mom was never satisfied with her efforts to do what was not her job in the first place. As an adult in her marriage, Fiona found herself doing the same thing—always being vigilant to discern what her husband needed and, as it was with her mom, never feeling adequate to the task.

There are so many ways children can be wounded. Most parents were doing the best they could with the comprehension and conditions they had. Given everything I've written, I obviously believe we all have been wounded. Further, I believe the stuff that occurs in our childhood is the raw material out of which we create the gold of our lives. I write this as one whose stuff was extreme; of course, I would not wish it on anyone. Yet by the time I was thirty-one years old, I began to view my life as an adventure, one that required attention, comprehension, and healing emotionally, relationally, somatically, and spiritually. I have many young friends who were born and reared into the most fortunate of circumstances: prosperity and parents who adored them. Yet they too face challenges; they too have plenty of work to do in the process of becoming whole.

Needs of Children

As any good gardener will tell you, a simple plant requires certain conditions and ingredients for its optimal development. If the plant doesn't receive what it needs, its bloom will suffer. Just so, from conception, children require quality tending for optimal development. It begins with gestation and birth. Both events can have profound developmental consequences.

Mom's state of being throughout her pregnancy affects the

quality of the fetal environment. Is she delighted to discover she is pregnant, or is she distraught? Does she have the support of her husband and family, or does she feel alone in her new adventure? Is she confident that her family's finances can handle the new addition, or is she thrown into a state of anxiety? Does she have the knowledge and firmness to avoid alcohol, tobacco, and other toxins, or does she have a "What's the difference" attitude? Does she look forward to the enormous commitment of childrearing, or is she feeling dread? The fetus is not impervious to these factors.

Dr. Frederick Wirth devoted his medical career to prenatal parenting. In his book *Prenatal Parenting,*[2] Dr. Wirth describes the many factors besides drugs, tobacco, and alcohol that can affect the life of a fetus. He discusses the effects of stress, negative self-talk, negative emotions, and the quality of relational support a woman receives from her family during pregnancy.

From the moment of conception, our genes are interacting with our environment. How they are expressed is influenced by the environment in which they are expressed. For example, a child born with a genetic propensity for introversion can, with support, learn to be social enough. This child may never become an extrovert, but with care and support, he can learn to socialize and enjoy people. In an unsupportive or hostile environment, beginning in the womb, that same child may be so painfully shy that any peer engagement is next to impossible. This interaction of genetic expression and environment begins in the womb and continues throughout life.

The Importance of the Birth Process

Birth is a profound transition; it sets an imprint upon which all future experiences may be shaped. Many years ago, Otto Rank, a psychoanalyst and an early student of Sigmund Freud, hypothesized that birth has a strong effect on the personality. Not very many of his colleagues agreed with him, and the concept fell by the wayside for decades. However, in recent years, a great deal more attention is being paid to both the birth experience and factors that influence intrauterine life.

One way to think about the birth experience is that it creates a template, a structure of expectations, for how transitions in our lives will proceed. Of course, the template will be substantially modified by subsequent experiences, but if those early experiences in some way reinforce our birth experience, then a very firm foundation of expectations is established. A traumatic birth followed by years of warm, loving, and attentive caretaking will produce results different from a traumatic birth followed by years of poor caretaking or maltreatment. Deeply ingrained patterns of expectations can very well have their roots in the quality of our birth. For example, a newborn who is not truly welcomed into the world and who grows up in a somewhat rejecting environment is likely to carry expectations of not being wanted.

During the process of birth, we are exceptionally vulnerable to serious impacts. If you had a breech birth or if forceps or vacuum extraction were used, the effects could be substantial. Interruption of the birthing process can also have consequences. Preplanned cesarean births have become quite popular, and in some cultures, Brazil for example, they are now routine.[3] According to Kristi Ridd-Young,[4] president of the Midwives College of Utah, currently 34 percent of births in the US are cesarean. Yet going through the birth canal and participating in the struggle to arrive is a design of nature. It is important. In my opinion, interfering with it simply for the sake of convenience smacks of hubris.

Incubation of the newborn or adoption can also have profound impacts. One woman in my practice was adopted at birth and was never told that her new family was not her birth family. For twenty-six years, she felt like she never fit in, just didn't belong. Finally, the secret slipped out, and at long last, she began to understand the feelings that had so haunted her during her lifetime. Another young woman remembered that she had been incubated for two weeks immediately after birth and was not allowed to be touched except with rubber gloves. For years, she felt that she was relating to people through some impermeable substance (like glass) and had difficulty getting close to people. In short, during the birthing process, as well as during the time immediately following birth itself, patterns can be established that affect an entire life. On occasion, a client with a relatively benign childhood is mystified by the challenges she has faced in life, and deeper inquiry suggests that birth impacts are a plausible explanation.

My mother was extremely upset to learn she was pregnant in late summer of 1942. Just a couple of weeks earlier, my father received word that his battalion was about to be shipped overseas, and the prospect of being a widow with a child haunted her. Her anxiety and tension must have contributed to an extremely difficult labor with the umbilical cord choking me as I exited. The story she told was that a very skilled obstetrician saved my life. To this day, I loathe tight-collared shirts and ties, and the issue of "Am I wanted?" still has vestiges of visibility in my consciousness.

Is there a story about your gestation and birth? What do you know about how things were for your parents during your gestation? Was your delivery easy? Were there complications? Was your birth cesarean?

Over the years, I have become convinced that many seemingly intractable patterns that human beings struggle to change have their roots in gestation and birth. Just knowing your story can be very helpful in bringing you more self-compassion. When the roots of an issue seem intractable, self-compassion is often among the best remedies.

Not all psychologists and psychiatrists accept gestation and birth as having significant effects on a person's life, but they all agree that the next few years are critical in forming who we become. A great deal has been written on how those years affect our personality, and in recent years, a great deal has been written on how our brains are affected by early childhood experiences.

Presence: An Essential Human Nutrient

We all agree that children need love. No one would deny that love is a fundamental need. But what does that really mean? People will say, "Of course I love my child," but is that sufficient? There was a time when food, shelter, discipline, and moral guidance were thought sufficient. In fact, the way we have generally thought about love is in terms of commitment, care, guidance, kindness, and so forth. I do not mean to diminish these in any way. They are important and necessary. However, we are realizing that they are not enough.

Human connections—and especially love connections—are almost as essential for the infant as food or air. We humans cannot survive without it, and we require it in good doses. It provides the ground for the growth of all other positive human qualities. Ideally, out of our very first connections, a sense of basic trust is born. Basic trust is trust in the benevolence of self, others, and the world. A reliable, stable, enduring sense of connection gives us trust that our basic needs will be met, that our food, warmth, care, and contact will be provided reliably. As trust grows, it bodes well for how we navigate closeness to other beings throughout our lives.

Today, we know that it is not enough to simply say that a child needs food when assessing nutritional requirements. Just so, it is insufficient to say that a child needs love. What a child needs is a balanced diet—interpersonally and emotionally as well as nutritionally. What are those interpersonal nutrients that provide brain and heart with the substances needed to thrive? There are several that we all need as children. However, they all flow from *presence*.

"Being present" is the overarching requirement for meeting the needs of a child. "Presence" is not a simple concept to define. It refers to the quality and quantity of energy and attention that you bring to a situation or person. It is being available for a heart-centered engagement in which a person is "touched" by another's being. It is like a light from the heart that shines through your eyes and reaches the other, who feels it. In such a moment, there are no distractions. There is recognition of the other's "being."

A person who is chronically not present may love another person, but the other will rarely *feel* it. There will be a hunger, a longing for a quality connection that is not forthcoming. Here is another way of looking at presence. In a championship ski run, a competitor can be nowhere else in her attention. Every cell in her body must be focused on exactly what she is doing. This level of athletic presence is required for the course of the event. At the other extreme, imagine a ticketing agent looking at his Facebook page, watching the girls go by, and absentmindedly handing out tickets to an occasional customer. Presence exists along a continuum of this nature. Of course, people can be present with nature or in their sport or with things and at the same time be unable to be present with another human being. Real intimacy can be very frightening, and it requires two people to be present with each other. We will be saying much more about this in Part 2.

A skier must be able to adjust to the demands of the terrain. A parent must be able to adjust to the demands of the moment. Some moments call for warm empathy, some for consolation, some for fun and play, some for discipline, some for light conversation, some for wisdom, and so forth.

Here's another image to understand presence. Imagine a human being is an ornate chandelier with a thousand tiny light bulbs. Your degree of presence is the number of bulbs that can be lit at any given moment. My experience has convinced me that almost all of us can turn on far more lights than we suspect. You can learn to replace your burned-out bulbs with intention, practice, knowledge, guidance, and the resources provided in this book. When the bulbs are mostly lit, and when the glow passes from you to another, that is a moment of love. The presence of another human being is a gift. It's the transmission of love.

Not too many decades ago, a central motif of childrearing was that "children should be seen but not heard." And as is often the case with cultural mores, the pendulum has swung to the opposite extreme. Recently a patient complained, "Everything, absolutely everything we do, is for the kids. I just can't understand why they have never once expressed gratitude." Well, if the expectation is built in from day one that the world revolves around them, why would they express gratitude? It simply is what they have come to expect. Using our model of integration, we can say, "Everything is for the kids *and* everything is for the parents." Just as in the marriage, it's maximum individuality *and* maximum togetherness. This is never a static state; there's dynamic tension. As our awareness grows, we grow our ability to hold both while sometimes feeling the tug of one stronger than the other. This same model is applicable to freedom and structure. Children need all of them—structure, discipline, and freedom—all concomitant to their level of development.

There are many more specific needs children have, such as the need for safety, for affection, for quality attention, and for attunement and empathy, without which a child will not feel seen or understood. Good tending means meeting these essential needs. Most humans have had some of these needs fulfilled in childhood and others not fulfilled. When the scale tips in the direction of a majority of these needs not being met, the scale registers poor tending. As a consequence, we turn off some of our light bulbs, less it be too painful.

What You Can Do: Practices to Support Presence and Connection

While Walking

First, make an intention to practice presence for the next three or four minutes of your walk. As you begin, notice your mental dialogue. You are probably thinking about something that has occurred or will be occurring. Don't try to forcefully cut off your thoughts; instead, begin to sense the movements of your arms and legs. Soften your eyes and notice what they are seeing without labeling or describing them. Just take in the shapes, colors, objects, the landscape, and people. Do the same with the sounds. Just notice them. Notice the movements of your abdomen and ribs as you breathe. Feel the sensations on your skin, especially your face. Allow thoughts to come and go without focusing on them. Now gently follow your breath into your torso. Have it be a soft, gentle, easy breath, and notice how the tissues of your lower abdomen and lower ribs are responding. Try not to force it; it's an easy breath through your nose.

In Relationship: While Engaging in Conversation with Another

Naturally, when conversing, you will be looking at your friend, but for this practice, simply include yourself in your field of attention. The aim is to practice including awareness of your body, sensations, feeling tones, emotions, sense of spaciousness or constriction, and whatever else may be occurring within you as well. This is a feeling kind of attention, not a mental laundry list of what is occurring in you. The greater the degree to which two people can be with themselves in this way while they are with another, the greater the potential for a nourishing connection.

Become comfortable with eye contact. In the right circumstances, practice really seeing the other, be it a friend, child, lover, or parent. Stay with their eyes for a second longer than you are comfortable with. The eyes are, as we know, the gateway to the soul, and it is your soul that wants to be seen. Many people are very uncomfortable with eye contact. Notice how it is for you. Practice taking that extra second to expand your comfort level.

Be generous with your acknowledgments and appreciation of your partner, children, and friends. Strive to create a positive environment for each relationship. Be generous with yourself.

Most people are much more likely to spend time criticizing themselves and very little time appreciating their good qualities or accomplishments.

Notes

1. Smith, Huston, *Why Religion Matters: The Fate of the Human Spirit in an Age of Disbelief*, HarperCollins, 2001.
2. Wirth, Frederick, *Prenatal Parenting*, Regan Books/Harper Collins, 2001.
3. This has been told to me by several friends in Brazil, including a pediatrician and an oncologist.
4. Ridd-Young, Kristi, president, Midwives College of Utah, Personal Communication, 2014.

3

Cultural Wounds

What does it mean to be a human being? Our ideas change over time. Slavery, for example, was part of the fabric of society for many centuries. Now the idea is abhorrent. No matter what era of civilization we enter, the population believes that theirs embraces the ceiling of understanding. Yet, there is so much more for us to learn. We are here on this earth to grow somatically, psychologically, relationally, and spiritually.

Who would argue that both individually and culturally we cannot improve our conflict resolution skills? Our interpersonal relationship skills? Our health habits? Our emotional intelligence? Our "in-touchness" with our own body? Our faithfulness to spiritual principles? It is in this sense I am saying we all share some degree of limitations and wounding. Further, just looking at the conventionally accepted wounds—addictions, anxiety, depression, poor physical health, marital distress, narcissism and more—we would still be shocked by the numbers. Or maybe we wouldn't, because surely, we all know someone suffering from one of these pervasive challenges.

What if we discovered that we are the ones making meaning

of our lives? That we are the authors of our lives? What if we could change the story we tell about our lives? Most of us have a rather fixed sense of who we are, without knowing that our sense of who we are is unnecessarily limited and confining. Opening up our sense of identity can be enormously freeing. Yes, we must develop an integrated sense of "I," but that "I" ideally will continue to evolve and expand throughout our lifetime.

Responsibility (or authorship), identity, and connections are three aspects of our lives I have chosen to highlight. Do I feel mostly in charge of my life, or do I feel I'm a victim of my circumstances? Do I have a strong core and a capacity to embrace the polarities of my being? Or is my sense of self rigid and fixed? How well connected do I feel to my body, to my own depths, to others, to nature, and to a superior power? A lack of cultural understanding, coupled with the impacts and insults of life, diminish us in all three of these areas. Let's begin with the issue of authorship or who is responsible for our lives. This can be tricky, so I'll begin with my own experience.

I could easily argue I was a victim of my family circumstances, given the physical and emotional abuse I received throughout my childhood. My father had a third-grade education in Italy, and my mother a sixth-grade education in New York City. My father rarely engaged with me and pretty much stopped talking to me when I was six. My mother began swinging at me as an infant. My beatings, as well as putdowns and humiliations, soon became an almost daily ritual. What terrible provocations did I perpetrate to warrant such a ferocious response? My number one crime was "talking back." There is absolutely no justification for their behavior. So *no,* I neither condone nor justify it. What I take responsibility for is the meaning I made of the abuse that occurred.

We all make meaning of the events in our lives. *The conclusions we draw for even the most heinous events that befall us are where we assume authorship.* The most likely meanings children will make from abusive situations such as mine are many of the ones I initially made: I was bad; I deserved beatings; I didn't deserve to be loved; authority figures will sooner or later hurt me; don't trust anyone to come close; they will only hurt me. These conclusions become part of our "felt-sense" of our body, our "felt-sense" of our self.

However, once we begin recognizing that we can take charge of both the writing and telling of our life story, thc potential for growth exponentially increases. I wasn't bad. I deserved to be loved. Later authority figures were not there to hurt me. My very childhood was the raw material out of which I crafted a life of meaning, service, and adventure. By the time I was in my early thirties, I began viewing my life as an exploration and journey; what a radical departure from my previous victim mentality! Unquestionably, I still had many issues and challenges to resolve. But holding them in the context of "I am the author of my life" makes for a completely different and so much more empowered life. Believing that we are simply the victim of our circumstances is a debilitating place from which to live our lives. Growth is virtually impossible.

The point of view that we are writing our own story and have always been writing our story is the most powerful position I can assume. Of course, things happen! Sometimes things that can only be described as horrible occur. Our lives may be completely disrupted by unexpected events. Huge challenges can emerge; tragedy may befall us. Yet how we respond, how we accept, how we reject, how we recover, and how we rebuild is within our domain. Yes, we may feel pain, hurt, fear, and anger. These are natural emotions. Yes, we may mourn and grieve. These are natural responses to loss! In no way am I espousing denial or suppression of feelings. But as feelings move through us, we can restore equilibrium. Emotions may come in waves, but as they pass, balance can be restored and we can focus on moving forward. This is not an original idea. It's found among ancient Greek philosophers, and it's found among great spiritual teachers as well. Recognizing this allows us to take more responsibility for our lives.

In the writing of our story, we forge our identity. We identify with, or claim, certain qualities, attributes, styles, and emotions. Some qualities are simply not relevant to us. But other aspects of self that can be relevant and useful, often are disowned. They are actually part of who we are, and they are important to our sense of wholeness. However, because they have not been supported or approved by our family or the culture we grew up in, we disown them. They become "not me." This process of reclaiming what we have disowned is an integral part of the journey toward our wholeness.

Again and again, we'll see the distinction between *either/or* versus *both/and.* The first constricts our sense of self and sets up the likelihood that the disowned energy will be projected onto another person or group. They then become the bad guys because they carry—in our minds—the qualities we cannot stand in ourselves. *Either/or* narrows our sense of self and reinforces our sense of separation from others. *Both/and* expands our sense of self and leads to compassion and understanding.

Throughout my early life, I disowned my own fierceness. My mother was the "fierce" one in our family. I was forever the nice guy, except when I had too much to drink. Then fierceness would erupt into bar fights. As I began to own this quality, not only were there no more fights, but I could stand up for myself, back myself up when I needed to, and cut through BS clearly and succinctly. The disowned fierceness was now a strength.

How many of us can embrace the fierceness of our animal nature? We are mammals, yet we are the deadliest species to ever live on this earth. Most of us act as if we don't have an ounce of aggression in our bones. What I am talking about is the ability to bring clarity and act with strong decisiveness when needed. It is the ability to not allow anyone to step on our vulnerability either unconsciously or deliberately. It's the wildness needed to not be normal, to try new things, to assert and honor our uniqueness. It's a great quality to have in the bedroom. When this quality is prohibited, suppressed, or simply not supported by family or culture, its energy twists into the force of our inner critic. Almost invariably, when we see a person with a very strong inner critic (as distinguished from a strong, clear, and supportive conscience), we will be looking at someone whose own sense of animal instinct has been stunted.

I imagine that when I speak of instinctual energy, it can sound frightening. In fact, it can be without the presence of "and." For example, we have mentioned tenderness and vulnerability. These qualities, along with spiritual sensitivity, balance beautifully with directness and strength. Without any of those balancing forces, fierceness can be antisocial, highly manipulative, or just cold and calculating.

Here is a story that makes the wound of identity very clear: Once upon a time, a pride of lions got caught in a vicious storm. A lion cub was separated from the group and later rescued by a herd of goats. The goats raised the lion, who learned to bleat, walk, and feel like a goat. One day an old lion was walking along and came across the lion behaving like a goat. He took him by the scruff of his neck and dragged him to the river, where the younger lion, seeing his image, realized he was in fact a lion. He began to roar like a lion rather than bleat like a goat.

And this is how it is with so many of us. Unless we are taken to the river of awareness, most of us will live and die believing we are goats. Most human beings are much more powerful *and* much more tender and vulnerable than they take themselves to be. Frequently, people will identify with one side or the other. For example, the super masculine man who disavows any feelings of vulnerability or tenderness. Or the hypersensitive, emotional female who is forever feeling wounded.

Intelligence is another area where much is disowned. We are much more intelligent than we take ourselves to be. Intelligence has been so narrowly defined until recently that it is still almost universally equated with academic intelligence (i.e., verbal-conceptual skills and quantitative skills). Who, for example, thinks of self-knowledge or interpersonal dexterity when they think of intelligence? Several other obvious dimensions of intelligence are also rarely considered. Harvard University Professor of Psychology

Howard Gardner outlined nine types of intelligence.[1] So many intelligent people don't realize their gifts. In these various ways we narrow our sense of self.

Now let's look at connection. Our connection to our own body is fundamental to our sense of connection to life. We can include the gracefulness of our movements, our flexibility, strength, and fluidity. It's our very sense of aliveness. It is the felt-sense of our own body, the importance of which we will address in depth in chapter 11. Both our guts and our heart have virtually their own nervous systems, with each being a source of intelligence and knowing. How well connected are we to them? There is also the connection to other people and other life forms. To borrow Fritjof Capra's term, we are part of the web of life. The notion that the rational mind is the universe's most superior and intelligent entity and all other life forms are just things apart from us to be studied and controlled is a prima facie absurdity.

We live in a time of rapid and profound change. Yet so many people become hopeless, anxious, or depressed. Incapable of making the necessary adjustments and adaptations, so many remain stuck in some level of unhappiness. We are more hyped up than ever and less capable of adjusting to changing circumstances. A deficit in our sense of connectedness challenges our ability to adapt. This is a wound of astronomical proportions—loss of connection.

Our connection to our spouse or life partner is clearly among the most important we have. It is perhaps one of the most challenging and satisfying dimensions of this adventure toward wholeness. The quality of this primary human connection depends—among many other things—on how well each person's nervous system functions. There is simply no way to have a healthy, vibrant, sustained intimate relationship without the ability to regulate one's emotions in the context of that relationship. We must be able to get thrown off center and recover. From the smallest of annoyances to searing moments of shame, it is necessary to feel and deal without going off the rails. Areas of rigidity or chaos within us are limiting factors in relational possibilities. What I am describing is fragmented or weak connections—to self or other.

We can learn to regulate our energy and emotions better so the ship of our marriages and partnerships can sail with greater tranquility and depth. We uncover new parts of ourselves, bringing more richness and excitement to our relationships. We learn to become open and transparent, living with honesty and integrity. We recognize the vibration of love and share it more generously.

Our very health depends on the quality of our connections. Every report I have read in the past few years ranks the US poorly in overall health statistics. Poor diet and lack of sufficient exercise are often cited as the reasons for this dismal picture. As much truth as there is in this assessment, it simply does not go far enough.

We are spiritual/relational/somatic/psychological beings, and every part of the whole must be considered, and every part affects and is affected by every other. Our connections don't stop at our skin or at our human relationships. There's more to the whole.

Throughout history, indigenous cultures most certainly had a very different relationship to the earth and sky. For many cultures, earth and sky were sacred. And why not? Life cannot exist without light, air, earth, and water. Holding them as sacred helps us feel connected to something beyond our egoic "I." It is the beginning of perceiving the sacred in our everyday lives. We live in a commodified world. Everything has become an object we can separate ourselves from, measure, and control. Recognizing and acknowledging our relatedness is the first step in knowing we are part of something greater than ourselves. It is also the way to experience a sense of the sacredness of our everyday lives.

Countless books have been written on developing an "abundance consciousness." The appreciation and reception of light, air, and water is the first step toward such a transformation. Forty years ago, I recognized some deep beliefs within myself about poverty being my lot, as it was for my family. Learning to value what I had and what was freely given was my first step toward transforming the pervasive sense of poverty as my destiny. The gifts of nature are most essential to our survival, and they are free. How well can and do we receive them? Can we be grateful for all that is given generously? The more sincerely grateful we are, the more we will have to be grateful for. My own life is a testament to this assertion.

So to be "wounded" in this sense does not mean to deviate from a statistical normal; it means to fall short of what's possible: our own beautiful unfolding uniqueness. It is possible to sense ourselves as the authors of our own life story while simultaneously feeling the presence of a Higher Power orchestrating our lives; it is possible to come to know ourselves as potential, with an evolving sense of "I" as both this fully embodied, feeling individual self, *and* a tiny speck of the web of life (from whence comes the virtue of humility); it's possible to deepen our connections above, below, and across. What other pursuit could be more rewarding?

Notes

1. Gardner, Howard, *Frames of Mind*, Basic Books, 1983.
   For example, *naturalist intelligence* can be considered nature smart. One of my teachers lived mostly alone for fifteen years in the Amazon forest. His ability to discriminate bird calls and animal sounds, to identify many species of plants and their usefulness, and to know when weather was changing or what was coming was truly uncanny. *Musical intelligence* can be thought of as sound smart. It's the ability to make fine discernments among sounds, to easily find pitch and rhythm, to learn music. *Logical-mathematical intelligence,* of course, is one of the academic intelligences that we have equated with "intelligence" for decades. So is *linguistic intelligence* or word intelligence, conceptual intelligence. *Spatial intelligence* is also measured on the standard intelligence tests and is an important quality for architects and others who deal with the relationship of objects in space. (Or for folks who like crossword puzzles). *Spiritual intelligence* is having a sensitivity toward life's important questions, such as "Why are we here? What happens after we die?" It is a predisposition to spiritual inquiry. *Interpersonal intelligence* is the ability to deal and act effectively with others. It

includes empathy, emotional understanding, and compassion. *Intrapersonal intelligence* refers to our degree of self-awareness. *Bodily-kinesthetic intelligence* refers to body awareness, coordination, and ease of learning physical skills.

4

Creating Our Reality: Core Limiting Beliefs and Sense of Self

The wounds of culture and childhood profoundly influence what we believe to be true about ourselves, others, and the world. How amazing to discover that much of the quality of our life and our relationships is influenced by what we deeply believe to be true. Limiting beliefs are at the roots of many of our challenges. Further, these beliefs are almost always formulated in early childhood, at birth, and perhaps even in the womb. They function as perceptual filters, allowing in what is consistent with them and keeping out what isn't. Discovering what they are is at the center of the adventure of healing and can change our life in a big way.

Long before a child utters his first words, he has begun to formulate beliefs about himself, others, and the world. These are implicit, emotional beliefs; they are prerational; they profoundly influence our sense of who we are. By the time we have reached the age of three or four, we have internally answered the following questions: "Are others dependable? Can I count on people? Is the world safe or dangerous? Will I reliably receive the nourishment and nurturance I need? How consistent are others? Can I trust? What happens when I express myself strongly? Are my emotions OK? Is anger allowed? Is my distress tolerable to others? Will I get help when I'm distressed? Is it OK to need? Will I be much better off if I focus on things outside myself and ignore my own feelings and needs? Is it OK to enjoy my body?" Obviously, these are important questions which can have a profound influence on our entire lives.

When a parent is able to notice that her infant is signaling a need, discern what that need is, and respond to it in a timely manner, she is positively affecting many developmental processes in the child. The baby is learning, "The world is a safe place. My needs can be met," "I am capable of making a positive change in my world," or "Other people are dependable and responsive. I can rely on people." These foundational beliefs influence and form the very core of how a child views herself and the world.

These considerations are not rational. As a two-year-old, we were not thinking about these questions. Nevertheless, we were drawing conclusions about them—emotionally—based on the kinds of interactions we were having with our parents and the quality of our environment. So, in the first three or four years of life, we begin to form our internal model of reality, which will continue to influence our perceptions, our behavior, and our body.

For example, if I have a core belief that people are not to be trusted, I will interpret a situation—say, being shortchanged by a merchant—differently than I would if I believe that people are basically trustworthy. In the first case, I might assume that the merchant was out to make a quick buck; in the second, I might assume it was accidental and give the merchant the benefit of the doubt. In the first case, I am more likely to be tense in the situation. With the second belief, I am more likely to be relaxed and see it as a nonevent.

Such limiting core beliefs will likely result in interpersonal distress or avoidance. They also will produce a heightened sensitivity to anything that confirms the negative perspective, which is another way of saying that your beliefs create your reality. If we are certain we will be rejected, abandoned or criticized, then we will notice and respond to every cue that could support that belief. The cues are evident and in clear view. Conversely, we will overlook, not see, or minimize those environmental cues or events that contradict our deep beliefs. In this reality, they will tend not to exist.

The model we generate of self, of other, and of our world is vital to how we function in life, vital to our relationships, vital to our successes and failures, and vital to our health. When important developmental needs have been chronically unmet or when we have received serious impacts or maltreatment, our core beliefs will generate pain and distress. They become rigid, unconscious, and therefore resistant to change. They are a chronic form of stress that compromises our vitality and whole-heartedness. We formulate these beliefs about our body, our lovability, our competence, our strength, our attractiveness, our sexuality, our food, and our money. In short, the whole of life is influenced by what we deeply believe to be true. Remember, however, these core limiting beliefs are just that: beliefs. *They are not the truth about who we are.*

Two Kinds of Dysfunctional Beliefs

There are two kinds of dysfunctional beliefs we human beings hold: beliefs that offer a positive outcome if we conform to expectations, and beliefs that offer no hope.[1] The less severe are the beliefs that offer a positive outcome; however, they are dysfunctional because they are conditional and lock us into a way of being that constricts choice. An example is a belief that the only way to be loved is to always be nice. I'm sure every reader of this book knows someone under the sway of that belief. It will bring rewards, but it will also constrict and limit one's sense of self, and it will limit one's ability for real emotional intimacy and honesty. If I can't let you see that sometimes I just don't feel "nice," then I can't be real and transparent with you.

Another example is "If I ever show anger, I will be abandoned. To be loved I can never show you my anger." This diminishes my sense of who I am and limits my intimate relationships. However, even though these are limitations and restrictions, they also offer hope. "Yes, I can be loved. I can be accepted, as long as I pay the price." There is a price, and it can be heavy and life draining, but at least there is a way.

More severe are the beliefs that offer no hope. An example is the belief "No matter what I do, I will never really be loved." Another is "Nothing I do is worthwhile." I may believe, "If I open up and get close to someone, I will be hurt," or "If I ever let my guard down, I'll be wounded." With these beliefs, there is nothing I can do to get what I need. I am doomed. Hopelessness, anxiety, or depression often follow. Much of human suffering is related to these pain-producing and limiting beliefs. Ferreting them out is an essential endeavor for sustained well-being.

I recall reading a book by Jane Roberts, *The Nature of Personal Reality*, in which she argues that our beliefs create our reality. At the time, I was working in a children's clinic where we had a playroom with a dartboard. For an entire year, I had been playing with those darts, and I had never put more than two or three of the six darts in the bull's-eye. As I was reading Roberts's book during lunch one day, I had a jolting realization: at my core, I believed that *nothing I ever did or could do was worthwhile*. My whole body felt the jolt. I stood up and threw all six darts into the bull's-eye! A core belief had come to light, and as we will see, bringing a core belief to light is the first step in changing it.

These beliefs are emotional constructions generated out of feelings of distress. When an infant or toddler's predominant experience is distress, when there are chronic insults or serious impacts, then "I feel bad" is how he comes to know himself. The "feeling bad" state gets embedded as "I feel bad; therefore, I am bad." Again, this is not a cognitive process. It's visceral. It is a felt-sense of self. It is a feeling of deep shame, and its effects can show up in many ways. For example, clients will reveal that they always felt they were somehow a disappointment to their parents, an inconvenience, or an annoyance. Rarely, if ever, will the child conclude that parents are not quite up to the task, that somehow their parents lacked some essential ingredients to do the job well. Almost invariably, they conclude they are flawed or defective. Sadly, and tragically, this lies at the core of so many human beings. It is a felt-sense/belief that keeps us from disclosing ourselves openly and honestly and makes the expression "Love yourself" seem like a foreign language. How can we love ourselves when at the deepest layers of our constructed "self" is this sense of "I am bad, flawed, or defective"? When I "know" I am inferior, unlovable, or unwanted? We must then always keep some part of ourselves hidden, and true intimacy becomes virtually impossible. These deep emotional wounds affect us as *whole organisms*, not just our "mind" and emotions or even the brain. They affect how we breathe, how we hold ourselves, how we relate, and how we move in and engage with the world.

The Child's Solution: Construction of an Image

Wounds of the many varieties we have described lead to core beliefs about ourselves, others, and the world. They are building blocks in the construction of a "self," not who we really are because, as we have seen, we are so much more loveable, powerful, capable, and intelligent than we typically take ourselves to be. But the pain of so many possible wounds is hard to bear. So we construct a solution. We create an image of self that we project outward so nobody can ever see how bad we feel about ourselves on the inside. We may become tough, rebellious, with a "nobody is going to hurt me" attitude. Or we may become super helpful. "I'll always be here for you, but I will never need anything." We may become rational and intellectual, always happy to share our thoughts and opinions. But feelings? What feelings?

These constructed images are not just the result of a mental or even just an emotional process. They are constructed with our whole somatic being and are intended to *protect* the very vulnerable, tender places that hurt to be seen. Real love—real, genuine connection from being to being—does not occur when we are relating image to image. Image-to-image relationships are hardly rare. An example is a couple I worked with who came in for therapy after she discovered he had been having an affair. As therapy progressed, she discovered she didn't know him below the surface. She was in love with his image. He was handsome, professional, athletic, and could take care of whatever needed handling. He had never learned to open up and reveal his deep feelings. It was only when he slowly became able to reveal what he really felt that she began to know him (and he her), and a real, intimate relationship began to form. This is an essential part of the journey I am advocating. It is a level of self-examination much too rare in our culture.

Who I am, or more accurately, who I take myself to be, is a malleable construction. Am I open to new information, or do I tend to live as a closed system? Am I pretty well-integrated, or am I clearly disintegrated? Do I tend to be rigid in my thinking, my attitudes, and my body, or do I display a level of fluidity? Am I expansive in my outlook, or is my worldview quite constricted? We come into the world with our genetic propensities and an anatomic gender. How that gender is treated in our families, in our subcultures, and in our society as a whole is a major input into our identity construction. Our race, ethnicity, and family religion further contribute in a major way. And, of course, there are our core beliefs, our operating principles. These beliefs, which *we begin to construct* from day one, furnish an unnoticed dimension to the elaboration of self.

Identity is one of the main dimensions in which we all have room to grow. We are so much more than we think we are! Astrophysicists tells us that every atom in our body originated in ancient stardust. We know our bodies are mostly fluid. At birth, we have the potential to learn any language on the planet. In other words, we are designed to learn, to grow, to change, and to adapt.

We can be powerful yet receptive. We can change shape, take in new information, and change attitudes, always growing in the direction of integration. However, as a result of the wounds of our lives, along with an insufficient comprehension of what it means to be alive in these human bodies and what we need, typically our sense of self gets truncated, rigid, and even fragmented. So much human suffering results from people identifying with only a small aspect of who we are.

The Jazz Band and Sense of Self

How does the jazz-band metaphor and "maximum individual freedom and maximum global cohesion" apply to our sense of self? Let's begin at the cognitive level. In a coherent personality, beliefs are self-supportive, not self-negating, self-destructive, self-minimizing, or self-aggrandizing. A person with a coherent personality is able to make a realistic appraisal of his strengths *and* weaknesses, with no need to diminish *or* inflate. Coherent beliefs are consistent with the fundamental reality of our nature and include self-acceptance *and* self-love.

Here is an example of how a sense of self is developed that does not necessarily bear a strong relationship to reality. As a little girl, my wife was always told she was a delicate child. Therefore, she was not allowed to engage in many physical activities—such as riding a two-wheel bike—until she was an adolescent. She was well into her adulthood before realizing she was anything but delicate. Yet she had a strong sense of herself as delicate, which was inculcated by parental propaganda and strongly influenced her relationship to physical activity.

A person with a coherent sense of self would have a fair amount of tolerance for ambiguity and what I call "and" consciousness, by which I mean an ever-growing awareness that we are multifaceted and multidimensional. *Holding paradox is a key to growth.* Here are some examples. A friend of mine has been in a relationship for about a year. A part of him is eager to commit and set the date, but another part isn't. Something "doesn't feel quite right." In a situation like this, my counsel is to make room for both parts. A part of him wants to be in this relationship *and* a part of him does not want to be in this relationship. It would be helpful for him to listen to what each part has to say and to assess how each part feels. The more fully he can embrace each aspect of self that is involved, the greater the possibility that the situation will flow organically, and clarity will come. A majority of our human suffering comes from our inability to embrace a bigger sense of ourselves.

What You Can Do: Practices

Ideally, at the center of self are beliefs that we are lovable, capable, and basically good, beliefs that the world is relatively safe, and others are fundamentally trustworthy, and perhaps with some effort, our needs will be met. We will be nourished and receive the love and attention we need. Of course, we all have some limiting beliefs. Discovering and changing them is among the major tasks along the journey of healing.

At this point, you might be wondering how to discover what you deeply believe to be true when, as I said, our deepest beliefs are often outside our awareness.

Honestly Reflect on the State of Your Life

Honestly reflecting about the state of our lives is one of the surest ways to ferret out what we believe to be true. If, for example, you have had a series of failed relationships, it would be valuable to examine what you believe to be true about yourself in relationship. The first step is to sincerely want to become aware of what is running the show of your life. Next, ask yourself to allow this to be revealed. Do not examine your challenges and conflicts from the point of view of your bad luck or it's always these other people's fault. Examine them constructively. Ask yourself whether you have some belief that is contributing to how these challenges and conflicts play out in your life.

By seeing them in the light of day, we take the first step toward challenging their reality and coming to see ourselves in a better, more expanded way. For example, if you realize that you believe you will be hurt if you let yourself get close to someone, you can test that belief. More than likely, the belief originated very early on in your life. You are not that child. You can bring new tools, comprehension, and skills into your current relationships. Once you uncover this core limiting belief, examine it closely. How does it manifest in your body? Imagine getting close and open with someone; sense what happens inside you.

When you have a good sense of how this belief manifests in your life, ask yourself, "Is this really true?" Take your time with this and see what comes up. Then ask, "What if the opposite were true?" With support from friends, you can test your beliefs in current time. "Will I always get hurt if I let myself get close? Do I do something that increases the probability of my getting hurt? What if I didn't do that next time? Might it go down differently? Do I choose people who bring a high probability that I will be hurt? In this case, what if you were deeply nourished if you got close to someone? Remember what was true in your infancy does not have to be true now.

Sometimes a good course of psychotherapy is the best way to reach these deep structures. Whatever orientation of psychotherapy it may be, it is likely to uncover beliefs you didn't know were there that were significantly influencing your life.

More Practices

1. Look for opportunities to insert an *and* after a position you hold or a view of yourself. Explore what happens. Notice sensations in your body. Notice any "voices" that emerge from your mind. All of this is useful information! See if you can locate within yourself some dimension of what you take to be *other*. An obvious example is "I am a man, *and* I have feminine aspects of myself. I can be receptive, yielding, feeling, and intuitive. In addition to the richness they bring, these qualities help me to empathize with and understand the females in my life." *And* is a simple three-letter word, but what a difference it can make!
2. As you discover limiting beliefs that are interfering with the fullness of your life, make a two-column list. On one side, write down a limiting belief you have discovered. Opposite it, in the second column, write down the belief you want to be true for you. Here's an example. In the left column, let's say the discovered limiting belief is "If I really open up with a man, he'll run away." In the second column, you might write something like "Even though a couple of men have left after I shared my vulnerability, many men would welcome an honest, deep relationship." This is the belief you want to construct; it's more in tune with reality because there really are many men who would welcome this. But if the first belief is operating, then you are likely to see and respond to the very first sign of a man shutting down and miss all the signals to the contrary.

Notes

1. Young, J., *Cognitive Therapy for Personality Disorders: A Schema-Focused Approach*, Sarasota, FL: Professional Resource Press, 1999.

Your Brain Requires Emotional Intimacy to Grow

What flows through your mind sculpts your brain.
Thus, you can use your mind to change your brain
for the better—which will benefit your whole being,
and every other person whose life you touch.
—Rick Hanson, *Buddha's Brain*

If we could point to one physiological condition causally related to all the following issues—addictions, chronic disease, chronic stress and worry, anxiety, relationship distress, divorce, loneliness, and violence—would we not want to devote considerable attention to its improvement? Of course, we would; the answer is obvious. The condition I am referring to is *insufficient development of our prefrontal cortex.**

* Some authors refer to the medial prefrontal cortex, some about the ventro medial prefrontal cortex. For simplicity I am referring to the prefrontal cortex when discussing which part of the brain is involved in the capacities I will be describing in this chapter. I owe much of the material in this chapter to a course I took with Daniel Siegel, whom I cite below. For an in-depth treatment of this top, see Dr. Siegel's, The Developing Mind.

Certain psychobiological and relational capacities require the development of the prefrontal cortex (PFC). With the development of these capacities, so many problems would be substantially reduced. Healing the wounds of childhood and culture and having the internal resources to thrive even in the face of adversity, requires a higher level of prefrontal cortical functioning.

It has been known for a long time that brain development is experience dependent. As children learn to distinguish shapes, sizes, distance, numbers, words, and concepts, their brains are fed and grow. However, only recently have we discovered that the qualities that make us most human, such as self-regulation, attuned communication, empathy, control of fear, self-soothing, response flexibility, self-reflection, a good moral compass, and the ability to trust your heart and gut feelings depend, in large part, on the development of a certain area of the brain. Further, for that area of the brain to develop optimally, emotional nutrients must be provided.

Attuned interactions, attention, empathy, affection, loving touch, structure, and acceptance are emotional nutrients we need for the development of our prefrontal cortex. What does it mean to be attuned? It means allowing one's feeling/vibrational system to meet another's. A mother quiets way down or revs up to meet her child where her child is. She's "there" with her child. Adults in intimate relationships do the same thing, as do good therapists with their clients. The experience that ensues is a powerful feeling of connection, of being seen and met. If a mother lives in too chaotic a state or too rigid a state, her ability to provide this essential nutrient will be compromised.

So in order for the following most human qualities to flourish, the prefrontal cortex must optimally develop, and for the prefrontal cortex to optimally develop, an ample amount of emotional nutrients is essential. The qualities are the following:

Self-Regulation

At birth, an infant lacks the ability to regulate his own feelings. Distress, delight, surprise, and anger are some of the basic, biologically based emotions that we express as infants. These different emotions come and go; they are up and down. The baby is dependent on Mother for regulation because he does not yet have the biological structures to do so. As Mother provides it to the best of her ability, the infant develops both the neurological and the psychological capacity to take on the job himself. The ability to regulate affect—excitement, energy, and feelings—is among the most important biopsychosocial skills a child must learn for adequate functioning in the world.

To understand this idea better, look at a thermostat. Whatever temperature it is set for, there is a small allowable range above and below. If it is set for sixty-eight degrees, when the room temperature drops below sixty-six degrees, more or less, the thermostat kicks in and turns the heat on. When the temperature in the room rises above seventy degrees, more or less, it does the opposite. What would happen if the temperature kept rising and the thermostat did not kick the heat off? Or what if the temperature continued to fall and the heat did not come on? It would be a problem. We rely upon the thermostat to regulate temperature for us.

Good regulation is the ability to regulate or modulate emotion—or our response to psychosocial challenges—and it is the foundation of a good life. When well-developed, self-regulation becomes the foundation for the growth of psychosocial competencies throughout our lives. When poorly developed, it leaves deep marks and renders us susceptible to a variety of stress-related difficulties.

Examples of Poor Self-Regulation

- inability to control our temper, which can be set off by the slightest provocation

- getting frustrated in a traffic jam and being upset for hours
- having a hard time restoring our spirits after a slight disappointment or defeat
- being upset for days after a difficult conversation or a confrontation

These are just a few examples. Some people's lives are so chaotic that they have a constant frenetic quality and can't calm down and relax. Others' lives are so constricted that they rarely venture beyond very narrow borders. They may be afraid to try anything new, afraid of change, afraid to venture into unfamiliar territory, and even afraid to travel. Not knowing what they might encounter, they don't want to risk having any feeling they can't manage or any situation that might derail them. Successful intimate relationships require adequate self and relational regulation.

Of course, most of us often don't acknowledge or even know what is really motivating our preferences. We don't say we are afraid to go on a trip because we don't believe we can manage the emotions that may arise. We put forth a more personally acceptable rationale.

Self-Regulation and Shame

Shame is a difficult emotion to deal with because it is accompanied by a desire to hide. Frequently, we don't even know that what we are feeling is shame. Our guts and the tissues of our face may feel tight. We may feel flushed and hot. Our perspiration may have a different odor. We may think we are feeling frustration or anger—or almost anything else but shame. Shame can be insidious, and because it is so dreadful to simply acknowledge and face, it is a difficult emotion to regulate. If we could simply feel it, name it, and express it, it would not be the insidious emotion that it is. When ashamed, we don't want to be seen. It's too painful. We feel defective or deficient. To address shame requires courage and a relationship in which there is great safety. It is the hardest emotion to deal with. Whereas guilt is associated with something I either did or did not do, shame says "I am bad, deficient, defective, and unlovable."

Biologically, as an innate affect, shame serves a purpose.[1] Here is an example: A toddler is excited and about to knock Aunt Sadie's favorite vase off her coffee table when mother emphatically says, "No." Not only was the toddler very excited, but he had been resonating positively with Mother and was expecting more of the same. That is, he was expecting Mother to match his increasing excitement as he reached for the novel and stimulating object. Mother's "mistuned" response deflated the child's high sense of excitement. This deflation is called shame. As Mother is able to attune to his experience, his energy returns and that rupture has been repaired. A few years ago, friends were with us for dinner along with their then two-year-old son, Vinay. As we were finishing dessert, Vinay, who was playing by our living room window, reached for the blinds, which would easily have come down if he had pulled them. In a moderately loud voice, I said, "Vinay, no!" His deflation was immediate. I had interrupted his excitement and interest. Fortunately, his mother's repair was just as immediate. She spoke to him with soothing words and made certain he knew that it was the action that was wrong, not him. As she did, I watched his energy quickly fill back up.

The infant is dependent on Mother's more mature structures to provide regulation. Two important events now occur. One is that the child internalizes these breaks in his excitement as stored images. Soon, he will be able to call upon these images in the absence of Mother and provide his own regulation. Second, regulation of these deflation and repair experiences literally helps important parts of the child's brain and nervous system to grow.

Although these repair transactions often have a verbal component, essentially, they are vibrational. The whole sequence can occur without words. It is critical that a child learns how to rebound from such a state. Recovering from moments of shame is a crucial aspect of effective self-regulation. The child is learning that he can come up when he is down and come down when he is up. He is also developing the neurological structures that will enable him to control the process himself. He is learning his caregiver is reliable and trustworthy.

Often, an individual who is deficient in this capacity will avoid close, intimate relationships. Relationships that involve removing clothing, sleeping with another, revealing our deepest fears and hopes, and being seen in our raw, more primitive moments all require us to regulate our affect. Certainly, there will be moments of shame or embarrassment, and if we can't quickly recover from their impact, we will tend to avoid situations that could potentially evoke these unwanted feelings. Self-regulation is a foundational capacity for healthy relationships and a healthy life.

Attuned Communication

The next capacity that requires the participation of the prefrontal cortex is the ability to *engage in attuned communication.* It is a wonderful feeling when someone is really with you. It is a feeling that the other is tuned in, connected, and being affected by you. They care about you. You can feel that he or she is there. You are not alone. People are starving for attuned communication, and sadly, few know it is what they are starving for. Having those moments when someone is so with you that their facial muscles are reflecting the movement in your facial muscles and their eyes are reflecting the feelings in your heart is something we humans long for. You can call it the experience of love. It is soul food for the brain, the heart, and the nervous system. Indeed, we pay a price when it is not provided. The capacity to provide this level of exquisite attention requires a well-developed prefrontal cortex, which means, of course, that someone provided it for us. It requires facial muscles that are free enough to express nuances of feeling.[2] If we have not received attuned communication, it is difficult to offer it. However, once again, it is never too late to improve and refine our capacity to be with someone in this way. Optimally, emotional nutrients need to be provided in ample quantity.

How do we achieve this higher level of functioning? It is by recognizing that from conception and throughout our lifetime, positive interpersonal emotional experiences provide the nutrients for the development of this area of the brain. From infancy onward, we need real feeling connections to thrive.

We now know that human beings are designed to learn and grow throughout their lives, not just in the first eighteen years of life. We have the capacity to change and learn. There were times in my twenties and early thirties when life looked hopeless. My habits were self-destructive, and my relationships were chaotic and seemingly futile. Too many human beings suffer in this way. Millions are in such straits. Yet it is possible for them—for all of us—to grow, to become more integrated, and to reap the rewards of the journey of healing. Change is possible because of the plasticity, resiliency, and growth potential of our brains *and*, as we shall see, of our entire body. We can become healthier—in body, mind, spirit, and relationships.

Empathy

Very much related to attuned communication is the next capacity that requires participation of the prefrontal cortex. It is the *ability to express empathy*. "I know, feel, and sense what you are experiencing, and I can let you know that I know." When you have an abundance of attuned communication and empathy in your life, you feel rich no matter what your circumstances. If you are not receiving these nutrients, you feel hungry, no matter how materially rich you may be. Like attuned communication, empathy is an essential nutrient, and it is my impression that most human beings are living with this nutritional deficiency.

Control of Fear

Fear is a fact of life. We humans are burdened and blessed with the knowledge of our mortality. A three-year-old is learning to master her fears when she play-acts that a scary monster is in her room and Daddy appears and saves the day. Adults are vulnerable, too. As much as we would like to think we're in control, deep down we know that life can turn on a dime. We may deny our fears. Many people do.

So if we don't want to repress or deny our fear, and if we don't want to let it run out of control, what options are left? There is a very challenging yet precious option. We can recognize and embrace our vulnerability as an intrinsic part of being human. We can feel the sweetness and poignancy of life and get to know it and appreciate it. We can protect ourselves without erecting impenetrable walls of defense. We can form a realistic sense of what we can control and what we cannot control.

Soothing

When my then three-and-a-half-year-old granddaughter was demonstrating her jumping twists from the sofa to the ottoman and back, she missed her landing and bumped her head hard on the edge of the ottoman. Of course, she wailed, but only for less than a minute as I held her and kissed her "boo-boo" to help the hurt go away. As children, we need others to soothe us. As this process becomes internalized, we learn to soothe ourselves. This doesn't mean as adults we shouldn't want to be soothed by others; it simply means we can develop the ability to soothe ourselves.

Countless situations require us to self-soothe. If our relationship breaks up, our lover or partner gets angry at us, a promotion we were expecting doesn't materialize, or we just had a bad day and are either criticizing ourselves or feeling criticized by someone else, these situations call for self-soothing. If we do it well, we are likely to tell ourselves something positive or optimistic, or we may simply attend to the part of ourselves that feels hurt and sad. We are able to let go of the frustration or agitation relatively quickly and return to a positive state. Without this ability, we are likely to indulge in too much food, alcohol, or drugs, watch too much TV, or play too many video games. All these behaviors are often efforts to soothe ourselves and feel better.

Response Flexibility

Response flexibility is the ability to respond instead of to instantly react. It means that between a provocation and our reaction, we can take a moment, count to ten, breathe, have a cup of tea, or take a walk. Taking that time means we can choose to respond differently than we would if we had just reacted in the moment. Developing this capacity also allows us to see different options instead of always doing something the same way. It takes a great deal of maturity to not react to provocations with blame and counterattack, especially when those provocations touch a vulnerable spot.

Self-Reflection

The next capacity is the *ability to self-reflect,* to examine our own behavior and see how we may have contributed to an interaction. So many people walk around feeling that they are life's victims. They blame others; they blame their circumstances; they blame God for their challenges and failures. What they rarely do is calmly ask themselves how they might be contributing to the situation and look for other options. Over years of working with people, I see over and over again the sense of empowerment that comes when someone realizes he has a choice in his situation and can develop the skills to engage those choices effectively.

A Good Moral Compass

If the opportunity presented itself to cheat on your spouse with a very attractive person, would you do it and do your best to cover your tracks? Would you do it if it were guaranteed you would not be caught? Would you refrain from doing it because you're afraid you'd be caught and the consequences would be brutal? Would you refrain from doing it because you could not imagine hurting your mate? Would you refrain from doing it because it just isn't right and you made a vow not to?

Clearly, the last two reasons suggest a more evolved moral compass. And once again, at the level of our neurobiology, a well-developed PFC is necessary to have a good moral compass.

Ability to Trust Your Heart and Gut Feelings

A few years ago, my wife and I moved to Salt Lake City to be near our family, especially our grandchildren. It was a major uprooting, and the transplant shock took several months to wear off. Before we left, a client asked how we knew it was the right decision. Immediately, I understood her question. I could easily imagine how difficult such a choice could be. In Seattle, my wife and I had so much: private practices, friends, church, community, and a beautiful home. It was a great question. Of one thing I can assure you: it was not a decision arrived at through a rational process. It was one of those instant moments of just knowing. It was a heart feeling and an inner knowing.

We all receive intuitive information. Whether we receive it as a heart feeling, a gut feeling, a sudden but clear image, or a sense of just knowing, it is information that we can learn to trust and value. Of course, we should then submit the "feeling" to a rational review, but we have the opportunity to cultivate those nonrational sources of information.

Obviously, a well-functioning PFC is at the heart of our

humanity. When it is chronically compromised, we have a situation where self-regulation, control of fear, attuned communication, empathy, self-reflection, self-soothing, a good moral compass, and trust in our gut and heart feelings are low. When we move along the continuum from poor tending toward maltreatment, we see situations in which the child frequently is left in distress. *The brain of an infant who experiences frequent neglect or maltreatment is exposed to intense states of biochemical imbalance.*

Evidence exists that when an infant is continually left in states of distress, without interactive repair, the result could be cellular death of areas of the brain that are involved in feelings and emotions. There is evidence that adverse social experiences can result in permanent changes in the brain's receptors for important neurochemicals. Changes in these receptors may be the mechanism by which intense stress leaves permanent marks on the growing brain.[3] My upbringing was clearly at the awful end of the continuum, and my life appeared destined to proceed along the trajectory in which it began. But thanks to God and some wise choices on my part—and some amazing teachers and friends—my life changed course and has continued in a positive direction. I now know in my bones and in my heart that, regardless of the hand we were dealt, it is eminently possible to take charge of our life and make it better. I can say unequivocally that life offers so much more than most of us ever imagined; the spiral of our life *can* turn, and it can *continue* in a positive direction. From conception and throughout our lives, positive interpersonal emotional experiences provide the nutrients for the development of the PFC. Ideally, those nutrients are present from infancy; however, it is never too late. Our brains will respond at any age.

What You Can Do: Reflections and Practices

Consider the nine capacities described in this chapter. Make note of where you want to see improvements in yourself. The practices listed in this book, and the recommendations made, all contribute to growing these dimensions in you. Here is an oldie but goodie: When you feel the rising heat of anger or rage, do not speak. Instead, focus your attention on taking a deep breath and begin counting to ten. Doing this takes willpower, but realize that letting the words fly in such moments only makes your life messier. Bring a quality of firmness and commitment to this practice. As you learn to stay inside your body, as you engage in difficult conversations—without anger or blame—you will feel your sense of power grow. And as your sense of power grows, you will get enraged less and less. The hot rage reflects a sense of powerlessness, a sense that you have no control in the situation. As you practice engaging in difficult conversations, your confidence in yourself will grow. As your confidence grows, explosive anger will recede.

Notes

1. For a thorough analysis of the origins and effects of shame, see Nathanson, Donald, *Shame and Pride: Affect, Sex and the Birth of the Self,* 1992. Also, Kaufman, Gershen, *The Psychology of Shame: Theory and Treatment of Shame-Based Syndromes,* 1996.
2. This notion that the muscles need to be free to fully express one's feelings will become clear in later chapters.
3. For an extremely thorough and in-depth examination of this, see Schore, Allan, *Affect Regulation and the Repair of the Self,* 2003.

6

Uncovering the Roots of Stress

To live a purposeful, rich, and engaged life without the insidious effects of intense or chronic stress is a worthy intention. It would be naive to suggest that life should always be free of challenges, free of tough moments, free of conflicts or upsets. However, it is possible to free ourselves from the chronic sense of fraying at the edges, feeling pressured, and fighting to stave off overwhelm. Too many live like this or use substances to avoid feeling like this.

Stress is a universal challenge in our culture and is important to understand. Few of us recognize the relationship between the wounds of childhood and culture, and our susceptibility to the negative effects of stress. We can chase symptoms, we can incorporate techniques of "stress- management," but to uncover the roots of stress, we must dig deeper. Further, since we now know stress is clearly linked to many if not most illness, it is imperative to ferret out the origins of our stress. In this and the next chapter we will understand what stress is, the mechanisms involved, and how it is related to our wounding and its profound effect on our health.

We have already seen how good tending in early childhood results in a strong and positive internal model of self. We have seen how real feeling connections are essential to the development of both psychological and neurological structures. These structures provide the foundation for resiliency, adaptability, health, and satisfying relationships. With a strong early foundation, an individual has the capacity to meet life's challenges—socially, interpersonally, and professionally. This does not mean that such fortunate individuals are immune to the disorganizing and painful effects of excessive impacts and insults that can occur later in life. It does mean, however, that they have a stronger base, a more secure foundation to which they can return.

Good tending is the beginning of a healthy lifestyle. *Children who are poorly tended, especially children who are maltreated, are more likely to deal with serious illness, both as children and as adults.* Those who are poorly cared for are much more likely to develop unhealthy habits of self-care. They are more likely to smoke, not eat well, not exercise, and drink excessively. They are more likely to have a less developed prefrontal cortex with all its accompanying challenges.

Many factors influence the quality of tending parents provide, including the following:

- the parents' emotional, spiritual, and social maturity, which inform their ability to be present with their children.
- their ability to discern their children's needs and respond to them in a timely manner.
- their everyday level of stress and anxiety.
- their comfort with touch, play, and sexuality.
- their love for each other.
- their own ability to handle conflicts well.
- their capacity to set firm limits and discipline with love.
- their ability to see others' uniqueness and honor others' individuality while maintaining a cohesive family unit.
- their ability and willingness to be available to engage, to guide, to teach, and to inspire their children.

Obviously, this is an ideal worthy of pursuit. What wonderful parents are those who can even come close to this. Looking at the continuum of tending, as we move away from the ideal, we find a large percentage of truly "good enough" parents, who raise wonderful, bright, and healthy kids. However, even in this cohort of wonderful, healthy, and bright kids, our culture offers far too few options and support in terms of identity, responsibility, and connections. The wounds of culture spare few. Now as we move even further away from the ideal, we find a large percentage of parents who, because of their own history and challenges, are emotionally unavailable and generally provide less than adequate care for their children. At the furthest end of the continuum we see maltreatment, neglect, and emotional, physical, and/or sexual abuse.

For decades, physicians dismissed any relationship between stress and disease because the physiological links could not be satisfactorily elucidated. Now, as the research grows, we can begin to comprehend the vital importance of human connection for the development of those physiological structures that support our health and well-being. As you are about to see, chronic stress contributes greatly to chronic disease. Furthermore, whether or not life's events enter our perception as challenges that we are ready and eager to tackle or as debilitating stressors depends on the foundation that has been established in the early years of life.

The prefrontal cortex is involved in self-regulation and serves a kind of executive function relative to our limbic system. Two structures of the limbic system I want to mention here are the *hippocampus* and the *amygdala*. The hippocampus is a small structure necessary to the formation of explicit, factual, or autobiographical memory. It is concerned with the context and sequence of events. The second structure, the amygdala, is tiny, almond-shaped, and lies deep under the cortex, close to the hippocampus. It assigns emotional significance to experiences and is important for processing highly charged events. It is our twenty-four/seven alarm center, always on the alert for threat or danger. It sets off the fight/flight response and carries emotional memory.

Here is an analogy of the relationship between the PFC and the amygdala from the world of business. Let's say a middle manager, in charge of a sales and marketing project, realizes that the plan he is implementing is not working. In fact, his data reveals that his company's competitors are getting an edge because his project did not do what he expected. Panicked, he tries even harder to make it work. However, his CEO has a bigger and better perspective on the organization, its competition, and the sector they are in. The CEO, who represents our PFC, counsels the manager, who represents our limbic system, to remain calm. Without operating from panic, he points out what needs to be done.

If the PFC is not well developed, the amygdala, which sets off the fight/ flight, operates without executive supervision, meaning it is much more likely to kick into fight/flight. So in addition to the compromised development of the qualities and capacities, such as self-regulation, attuned communication, and empathy, we are also subject to more frequent fight/ flight responses with less provocation than an individual with a strong foundation. More situations or events feel "stressful" more of the time.

Here is an example of a young man with a poorly developed PFC who responded with fight/flight in a situation most folks would see as innocuous. He had been having serious challenges in his life—including a brush with the law—and came to live with us. After eighteen months and some rather intense psychosocial education with my wife and me, and having completed his GED, he was ready to go off on his own and begin community college. He found an apartment with some other students. On the day of his move, we drove him to his new home. An attractive young lady answered the door and welcomed him. I found it fascinating to observe that he turned scarlet and the tension level in his face and neck skyrocketed as he struggled to find simple words like, "Hello, my name is..." In this case, the saber-toothed tiger was a young lady saying welcome, but his physiology didn't know the difference. Fight/flight had kicked in.

We will learn more about how the mechanisms of stress relate to health. In the human organism, these mechanisms represent an elegant and complex interweaving of the PFC, the limbic system, the autonomic nervous system, the cardiovascular system, the endocrine system, the immune system, and the neuromuscular and connective tissue systems. This is like an orchestra. Many different instruments play their part, yet they do it in complete harmony with each other. It is a beautiful arrangement. However, if one or more of the musicians is out of tune, the whole performance is affected. As in an orchestra, every aspect of our physiology, every system and organ, must dance in harmony with every other system and organ.

There is mounting evidence that stress is an influential factor in a wide variety of physical and emotional disorders. It has been estimated that the cost of stress-related disease is $200 billion per year.[1] This astronomical figure includes the cost of a variety of physical illnesses, such as heart disease, hypertension, asthma, diabetes, allergies, and other immune disorders. It includes syndromes, such as migraine headaches, fibromyalgia, chronic fatigue syndrome, and numerous digestive disorders.

There is a growing movement of medical educators who want to shift focus from treatment to prevention. To be effective, this movement toward prevention must understand and fully embrace all the factors included in quality of life and health. It is important to understand that feeling and believing that life happens to us without much agency—a sense of being a victim—is a source of stress. We must recognize that a limited and constricted sense of self means we don't have all the resources that are potentially ours, that a poor connection to ourselves somatically and emotionally contributes to our stress, and that the lack of deep emotional connection with another human being is a resource deficit, as is a lack of any sense of connection to nature. So yes, exercise, good nutrition, and stress management will indeed mightily contribute to good health, as long as we understand that healing the emotional, relational, somatic, and spiritual wounds are what provide the resources that enable us to handle life's challenges. What do we mean by the stress response?

The word *stress* may rank among the most commonly used words in the English language, yet from the very beginning of its usage, its definition suffered from vagueness and ambiguity. What exactly do we mean when we say we had a stressful day at the office? It could mean many different things. In its original sense as a physics term, stress refers to strain exerted on an object that can alter the shape of that object. In this definition, stress is a stimulus, an external force that affects an object or organism.

Stress also can be defined as a response—what occurs inside an organism as a result of perceiving a stimulus. More specifically, stress is what occurs physiologically when a situation or event is perceived as stressful, including its ensuing effects on internal or "target" organs. Target organs include the heart, brain, lungs, kidneys, adrenals, and pancreas. The mind can be a target organ, too. That is, stress can affect our perceptions, judgments, cognitive functioning, and even our personalities. In other words, our perception of an event affects our physiology and our psychology.

Understanding how stress relates to health and illness has been evolving over many years. The grandfather of that understanding was Hans Selye, a Hungarian researcher who was responsible for putting the word *stress* on the map. He was attempting to determine the effects of a particular hormone on the body. Lore has it that he was particularly clumsy in handling and injecting the hormone into his experimental rats, and periodically he dropped the little critters and had to chase them around to capture them again. When he conducted his examinations, he discovered that his experimental rats had peptic ulcers, shrunken immune tissues, and enlarged adrenal cortexes. Being a good scientist, he of course gave a neutral stimulus to a control group, so that he would not erroneously conclude the results he observed were a function of the hormone he had injected. To his chagrin, he found that the control group, the one where the rats had been injected with a benign solution, displayed the same responses as the group he had injected with the hormone. They, too, had ulcers, shrunken immune tissues, and enlarged adrenal glands. What was common to both groups of rats? Selye was handling both groups the same way. The effects were not from the hormone he was injecting, but from the handling process itself!

Daunted but not defeated, Selye wrestled with the problem. Finally, he arrived at the conclusion that there exists a nonspecific response to external demands—in this case, his handling of the rats. In other words, in response to any demand, the body has a *general stress response.* This is *normal, natural,* and *adaptive.* The organism's resources mobilize to meet demand, any demand. However, when the situation is prolonged, physical problems can occur. Selye termed this the *general adaptation syndrome.* The first response to threat is an *alarm reaction*; it is followed by a mobilization of resources, which he called the *resistance phase.* If the mobilization continues, resources are depleted. Selye termed this the *exhaustion phase.* In his theory, it was this exhaustion phase that resulted in illness.[2]

The stress response itself is a normal, adaptive, and healthy response to demand; human beings require challenges in order to grow and develop optimally. In this sense, stress is good. We need challenges, and we have the psychophysiological mechanisms to handle them. However, when the demand or impact is overwhelming and is too much for our resources, or when it continues for too long, difficulties will occur. To an infant or small child, receiving inadequate nurturing or having a parent who is not emotionally present much of the time is a very disturbing situation. For example, if the mother is depressed or a parent is chronically anxious, worried, and not very nurturing, the child will feel a chronic level of distress. Just being mishandled by a clumsy scientist was too much for Selye's rats. This simple example shows how the wounds of childhood are often a source of chronic distress. Stress plays a crucial role in health and disease, but there have been impediments to the general acceptance of that notion. As we begin to accept stress as a serious factor in health and disease, we may begin to take self-care more seriously than we have to date.

The major impediment to recognizing the complex role of stress has been 150 years of medical success based on the "one cause for one disease" theory. Another has been uncertainty about how stress translates into disease. For science to accept that A causes B, it is necessary to show exactly how that occurs. Until recently, how exactly stress caused disease was not well explained. Although it may be intuitively obvious that stress translates into disease, the mechanisms involved have been anything but obvious. Hans Selye's general adaptation syndrome described an "exhaustion" phase in which structures have been worn down. This was a beginning of understanding but hardly a sufficient explanation, even if it makes sense intuitively. Science requires more than intuition. Selye's theory just did not stand up to scrutiny, especially in the face of 150 years of one cause/one effect being "just how it is."

Several different theories have attempted to explain how stress translates into disease. For example, one theory—developed by a psychoanalyst named Alexander French—states that specific psychic conflicts result in specific conditions such as repressed hostility resulting in migraine headaches. Again, although there are certain conditions under which this theory might seem to have intuitive validity, it simply does not meet scientific standards.

Another theory states that individuals are genetically predisposed to respond to stressful stimuli with a particular pattern of psychophysical reactivity. If, for example, an individual is born with a "weak" stomach, under stress, it will be his stomach that is most affected by stress. In other words, when a specific organ has a genetic weakness and there is frequent stress activation, that organ will be the one to suffer first. Once again, this particular theory of translation makes intuitive sense but fails to account for all the data.

Yet another theory proposes that disease is not the result of direct stress but of insufficient motor expression.[3] This view suggests that our sedentary lifestyle is to blame for how stress translates to disease. These scientists point to the fact that the role of our musculature goes far beyond locomotion. It is well known that our striated muscles have a role in circulation, metabolism, and endocrine balance; they also serve as outlets for our emotions and nervous responses. Thus, it is conceivable that the great loss of mobility that has occurred over the last hundred years could be responsible for stress resulting in disease.

All of the above theories probably contain a degree of truth. Some cases of stress are due to the wear-and-tear effect, others show the effect of a predisposition for certain organs, and in yet other cases, the culprit is the great spread of a sedentary lifestyle. However, none of these explanations alone is sufficient to explain the phenomena to scientists' satisfaction.

Limbic Hypersensitivity Phenomena: A Common Denominator

Synthesizing decades of theory and research, a couple of Harvard psychophysiologists[4] arrived at a model that elegantly explains the pathogenic mechanisms in diseases that are considered related to stress and emotional challenges. The basis for the model was a consistent observation that certain technologies resulted in a greater capacity for relaxation and ameliorated or at least lessened the severity of a wide variety of diseases. These were technologies, such as meditation, biofeedback, and yoga. Since learning to relax can improve a wide variety of psychosomatic conditions, it seemed to follow that those conditions have a common denominator. Reviewing the experimental and theoretical literature, researchers concluded that the common denominator condition was something they called *limbic hypersensitivity phenomena, a state the limbic system is either chronically "aroused" or has such a low threshold that it is easily aroused.* This condition gives rise to a wide variety of physiological and emotional disorders. Discovery of a latent condition that can manifest clinically in a plethora of physical and psychological disorders has obvious and profound implications for prevention and treatment.

This limbic hypersensitivity theory accepts what is common to all previous attempts to explain the linkage from stress to illness: organs that are overstimulated for long enough eventually manifest disease. The dysfunction may be a result of wear and tear, biochemically induced trauma or toxicity, predisposed organs, or visceromotor fatigue or exhaustion. All of those explanations have some validity. However, *this model places its emphasis on the limbic system itself.* It states that a wide variety of etiological or causative factors—including emotional, cognitive, environmental, social, and biochemical—can result in limbic system-based neurological hypersensitivity. In turn, this state activates a variety of stress axes, such as the neurological, neuroendocrine, and endocrine axes, that can, through their effects on target organs, manifest as disease.

Limbic hypersensitivity phenomenon is a common denominator factor of a wide range of conditions that can be called arousal disorders.

Included in this classification would be all anxiety-related and stress-related conditions, both physical and psychological. Physical illnesses can include gastrointestinal disorders, such as peptic ulcers, ulcerative colitis, irritable bowel syndrome, and esophageal reflux; they can include cardiovascular disorders, such as essential hypertension and coronary artery disease; they can include respiratory disorders, such as asthma and allergies, and they can include many other disorders, such as migraine headaches, fibromyalgia, chronic fatigue, and chronic pain. Anxiety-related disorders include panic syndromes, generalized anxiety, and post-traumatic stress. It is also likely that many forms of depression involve limbic hypersensitivity phenomenon. The implications of understanding limbic hypersensitivity cannot be overstated.

Recall that the prefrontal cortex is a regulator of the amygdala, which sets off the fight/flight mechanism. We have examined the consequences of not having essential needs met—and especially of severe wounds and impacts—for the development of the prefrontal cortex. *This is one route to limbic hypersensitivity.* In the next chapters, we will look at other routes to this same phenomenon and take an in-depth look at what I mean by the quality of tissues. Here I will simply say that the skeletal muscles play a critical role in sustaining an aroused limbic system. The Harvard scientists Everly and Lating reviewed research showing that individuals suffering from any one of these stress-related disorders had higher levels of chronic muscle tension in their bodies. They concluded that *chronically contracted muscles bombard the limbic system and perpetuate its functioning in a high state of arousal.*[5] It is a circular process. Stress and anxiety lead to chronic muscle contraction. The biochemistry involved in chronic muscle contraction bombards the brainstem, limbic system, and cortex, thus sustaining limbic sensitivity.

I believe that the effects of stress in our culture are revealed in medical statistics, in the high prevalence of anxiety and depression, in the general malaise that many endure, in the divorce statistics, and in the relationship challenges many of us face. *The chronic stress of growing up feeling unsupported, harshly criticized, not emotionally well-nourished, or just not well-tended are significant contributors to this situation.*

Neurogenesis and Neuroplasticity—Positive Change Is Possible

Neurogenesis refers to the brain's ability to grow new cells throughout its lifetime. Scientists did not accept that this was possible until the end of the twentieth century, when a scientist by the name of Elizabeth Gould[6] demonstrated that the adult rat continues to produce new cells in an area of the brain called the *dentate gyrus*, which is part of the hippocampus. She also found that increased levels of cortisol and stress could suppress the production of these new cells, putting the process on hold.

Neuroplasticity refers to the brain's malleable, responsive, and resilient nature. In the process of learning, the brain actually remodels and reconfigures its very structure. Both neurogenesis and neuroplasticity are central to learning and memory processes, and both are put on hold in times of stress. This is a protective feature and another example of the adaptive nature of those stress mechanisms. If the stress is terminated, then both neurogenesis and neuroplasticity resume and there is no permanent damage to the brain. However, when the stress situation is chronic, protection becomes damage; a temporary restructuring becomes diminished connection or shrunken tissue. Just these facts should be enough for us to take stress seriously. Fortunately, research and my personal experience have shown that positive changes are possible even when the effects of stress have been severe.

We must understand and deal with our organism as a whole when seeking healing and realization of our full potential. I have already shared with you a little of my history, so it should come as no surprise that I was not a healthy youngster. At age three, I started getting migraine-type headaches, nausea, and all. By the time I was in my late twenties, I was getting severe headaches three or four times per month. They were the awful ones during which I sometimes tried to vomit just to get a respite from the throbbing pain. In addition to these, I also got several less severe headaches. That was a lot of headaches!

Looking back, it is hard to believe how low my energy usually was. Fatigue accompanied me everywhere, even as a child. And why wouldn't it? Beginning when I was a young child, I preferred cream pies and coffee (with sugar) for breakfast, followed by numerous candy bars and caffeinated soft drinks throughout the day. I loved to play, but by the time I was sixteen, exercise meant standing on the curb and sticking my thumb out for a hitchhiking adventure, and I was smoking over a pack of unfiltered Camel cigarettes every day. Of course, these factors don't include the chronic, insidious stress of an organism so incoherent and so unfulfilled in basic emotional needs. In my thirties, thank God, I began to change.

Notes

1. For readers wishing a more in-depth treatment of stress, I highly recommend the work of Bruce McEwan, *The End of Stress as We Know It,* or George Everly and Jeffrey Lating, *A Clinical Guide to the Treatment of the Human Stress Response.*
2. For an in-depth treatment of Hans Selye's work, see McEwan's *The End of Stress as We Know It.*
3. Everly, George and Lating, Jeffrey. *A Clinical Guide to the Treatment of the Human Stress Response.* (Note: pp. 50–60 describe the attempts to relate stress to disease.)
4. Ibid.
5. Everly, George and Lating, Jeffrey. *A Clinical Guide to the Treatment of the Human Stress Response.* New York: Kluwer Academic/Plenum Publishers, 2002, 182.
6. Gould, Elizabeth, et al. (1998), "Proliferation of Granule Cells Precursors in the Dentate Gyrus of Adult Monkeys Is Diminished by Stress." *Proc. Natl. Acad. Sci. USA*, 95, 3168–3171.

Stress and Health

> If I told patients to raise their blood levels of immune globulins, no one would know how. But if I can teach them to love themselves and others fully, the same change happens automatically. The truth is: love heals.
> —Bernie Siegel, MD

On August 13, 2012, the *New York Times* reported the death of Dr. William C. Reeves. He was sixty-nine years old. From 1992 to 2010, he directed research at the Centers for Disease Control and Prevention in Atlanta in one of the most contentious subjects in contemporary medicine: chronic fatigue syndrome. The article went on to say that at least 1 million Americans suffer from the syndrome, which includes severe fatigue, muscle soreness, difficulty concentrating, and sleep problems—*and* it has no known cause. For years, Dr. Reeves searched for the cause, for a virus or bacteria responsible for this affliction. According to Dr. Thomas Folks, a colleague, "He tried desperately hard to find the etiology, whether it was physiological or an infectious disease or whatever." When Dr. Reeves began to suspect that stress and a history of physical, sexual, or emotional abuse were contributing factors, he incurred the anger of many patients.

Why would people get angry when told that their problem might have stress or abuse as a contributing factor? The answer is not necessarily simple. First, patients know that they are genuinely suffering and that the suffering is in their bodies. Second, if stress and abuse are contributing factors, that might mean that the problem is "in their heads," which is not an acceptable diagnosis when the pain is clearly something they feel. Third, if stress and childhood abuse are factors, and the problem is systemic, there is no easy, tangible cure. No single medication or surgery is going to solve the problem.

How can we understand and address this? What gives? What gives is recognizing that the suffering patients are absolutely correct. The problem is in their bodies; the difficulty is with the medical model. For years, the medical model has ignored the possibility that mind and relationship factors can cause physical symptoms. And even the words *body* and *mind* are misleading.

From a physiological perspective, a general, nonspecific response to a wide variety of stimuli did not seem to make sense. Scientists had believed that a specific response always has a specific stimulus, and certainly they had believed that specific illnesses had specific causes. The nineteenth-century German physician Robert Koch, in fact, won a Nobel Prize for the discovery of a specific agent (the tubercle bacillus) as the cause of a specific illness (tuberculosis), greatly advancing medical research based on the theory of disease specificity. Hans Selye's groundbreaking theories were the major takeoff point for years of research on stress, leading to the radical concept of a common denominator cause for a variety of illnesses: limbic hypersensitivity. This was a new way of thinking.

Now let's take another look at the stress response and how stress affects different organs and systems of the body. Stress can be a factor in most diseases. Armed with this knowledge and an understanding of the root causes of stress, you will be better prepared to engage the practices and disciplines described in this book.

When the stress response is initiated, the organism's attention shifts from long-term needs to short-term needs. For example, reproductive or digestive activity is placed on hold. It's not important in the moment. The neuromuscular systems, however, require an increase of energy. The body is preparing itself to meet a demand, challenge, or threat.

The stress response can be examined along three different axes: the neurological, the neuroendocrine, and the endocrine. If you are interested in the physiological details of these responses, I refer you to Everly and Lating's book.

The Neurological Axis

The neurological axis is the response of the autonomic nervous system (ANS). It responds immediately when a threat is perceived. This system is so important to our understanding of stress, health, trauma, relationships, and body tissues that we will devote the entire next chapter to it.

The Neuroendocrine Axis

The neuroendocrine axis begins in the limbic system area of the brain. French surgeon and neuroanatomist Paul Broca first identified a group of organs in the brain that he referred to as the limbic brain. The word comes from the Latin *limbus,* which means *edge, margin,* or *border,* and it refers to an area above the reptilian brain that is common to all mammals. This area of the brain is at the center of activities dealing with stress, emotion, love, and trauma. The amygdala is the structure within the limbic system that initiates the neuroendocrine axis.

I recall a patient who tended to flare up intensely whenever anyone got upset with her or challenged her. A quality of rage would appear seemingly out of nowhere. This was her sensitized amygdala in action. That is its job—to warn when danger appears and set into motion our readiness to fight to the death or run like hell. Simply understanding that it was her over sensitized amygdala, allowed her to learn to tame the rage, causing it to dissipate in seconds. Later, as her prefrontal cortex became more engaged, her ability not to flare at all (i.e., to regulate her amygdala) grew.

The amygdala signals the adrenal glands, which outpour adrenaline. Adrenaline is one of the two major stress hormones; cortisol is the other. Adrenaline steps up the heart rate and sends more oxygen to the lungs, brain, and muscles. It stimulates secretion of a substance called fibrinogen, which aids in the clotting of blood. If you are preparing to fight or run, you may get wounded. How brilliant is the body to begin clotting your blood—just in case! It also mobilizes the release of glucose and fatty acids from their storage as glycogen and fats, respectively.

Adrenaline also increases blood pressure, heart rate, and cardiac output; it decreases blood flow to the kidneys, skin, and gastrointestinal system. Action requires energy, so these physiological activities mobilize energy in preparation for action. The whole body is made ready to engage the situation. This is not a condition to wish for except in the very short term to meet an emergency, which is exactly the design. However, when some of these effects become chronic, then the very systems designed to empower us suffer unwanted consequences.

The Endocrine Axes

Neural stimulation of the adrenals occurs rapidly. Slower, more prolonged effects occur along what are called endocrine axes. For a more detailed look at these, I refer you to books by McEwan and Everly and Lating. For our purposes, it suffices to say that cortisol is released via a sequence of hormone secretions and also comes from the adrenal glands. As with adrenaline, the effects of cortisol are both complex and double-edged. One of cortisol's first functions is to replenish the energy supply depleted by the effects of adrenaline. It does this by converting a variety of food sources into glycogen and fat storage. Too much or too little of either cortisol or adrenaline can tip the system out of balance.

For almost forty years, scientists have posed questions concerning the relationship of brain, behavior, and the immune system. This field came to be known as psychoneuroimmunology, and it has generated a vast amount of research. The basic question we are concerned with here is this: does stress affect the immune system? If it does, it must be considered in relationship to a host of infectious, degenerative—as well as so-called psychosomatic—diseases. In addition, if severe early wounding in childhood seriously compromises the healthy stress response, and if that, in turn, suppresses the immune system, then the link from early wounding to infectious, degenerative, and psychosomatic disease is established.

In fact, the immune system is an active participant in the stress response. Immune cells are generated in the bone marrow and are carried in the blood; they destroy whatever does not "belong" to the body. When the fight/flight mechanism is engaged, the chance of injury resulting from fighting or running away increases. Therefore, the immune system must prepare to deal with infection in case there is a wound. Initially, cortisol boosts the immune system by sending white blood cells to their battle stations and then turning off the immune response once an appropriate level is reached. Cortisol also shuts off its own production to keep the stress response from getting out of hand. So when a threat is perceived, cortisol sends out the troops, and if they don't find infections, they return home. When the threat is over, when the stressful stimulus goes away or is satisfactorily dealt with, cortisol sends an all-clear signal to the immune system. This is the sequence of events when the system is functioning effectively and in harmony.

If the protective functions of cortisol are not effective, such as when the perceived threat does not get resolved, the immune system can go into overdrive. Inflammatory and autoimmune disorders are conditions that arise when the immune system gets out of hand. In inflammatory disorders, the immune system goes on the attack in response to stimuli that do not bother most people, such as pollen or dust. Allergies are an example of the immune system on overdrive. In autoimmune disorders, immune cells fail to distinguish self from nonself, similar to what happens in inflammatory disorders, but they carry it one step further and begin attacking healthy tissues. Rheumatoid arthritis and type 1 diabetes are examples. In type 1, or juvenile diabetes, the immune system destroys insulin-producing cells in the pancreas, which results in dependency on insulin injections.

We begin to see how early impacts and insults play havoc with your immune system, setting the stage for a wide range of physical and/or emotional challenges. When our immune system is depressed, we are more likely to get ill. Numerous studies have demonstrated that emotions affect our immune system. In one study[1] with medical students, researchers demonstrated that loneliness could suppress the immune system. They also found that people caring for spouses with Alzheimer's disease without much social support fared worse in tests of immune system activity than did those with stronger social support.[2] Confirming an experience common to most of us, one scientist found that people were more likely to catch colds during periods of prolonged stress.[3]

In the early 1950s, 126 healthy men randomly chosen from their Harvard graduating class were asked to describe the closeness and warmth of their relationship with their mother and father. They were asked to choose among four answers: very close, warm and friendly, tolerant, strained and cold. Thirty-five years later, 100 percent of the men who had rated both parents low in warmth and closeness had been diagnosed with diseases, compared with only 47 percent of those who had rated both parents as high in warmth and closeness. The researchers concluded that the perception of love might turn out to be a core biopsychosocial-spiritual buffer, reducing the negative impact of stressors and pathogens and promoting immune function and healing.[4] More and more studies are revealing that an emotional dimension contributes to chronic illness. Previously, I mentioned the hippocampus, a small structure in the limbic area that is involved with memory. It is rich in cortisol receptors, and cortisol is a major stress hormone. The hippocampus is involved in the formation, organization, and storage of memories. Cortisol participates in that process. Stress hormones assist in engraving experiences into our memory. This is why we tend to remember situations in which we are emotionally involved. This is another example of the adaptive utility of the stress response. However, when stress levels are severe or exceptionally prolonged, the hippocampus itself and its role in memory formation are at risk; excessive or chronically elevated levels of these same hormones can damage this structure of the brain that is responsible for memory formation.

I can't help but wonder how much stress is involved in the development of dementia and Alzheimer's. In response to stress, the brain puts *neurogenesis* and *neuroplasticity* on hold. This is absolutely fine for a very short time; it is nature's design. However, these mechanisms, which are designed to protect us, turn against us when stress is excessive or prolonged. The wounds of culture and childhood play a significant role in our health and well-being. Our relational capacities, our model of self, and the quality of our PFC and limbic system are all entwined.

The statistics on cardiovascular disease in America are daunting. According to the American Heart Association, it is the number one cause of death in the United States, claiming the lives of 40.6 percent of the more than 2.3 million people who die each year. Almost 61 million Americans have some form of cardiovascular disease, ranging from congenital heart defects to high blood pressure and hardening of the arteries. According to the Centers for Disease Control and Prevention, about 600,000 people die of heart disease in the United States every year. That means one in every four deaths. Heart disease is the leading cause of death for both men and women. Every year, about 715,000 people have heart attacks. As with so many contemporary diseases, modern medicine has been brilliant in developing pharmaceuticals and surgical procedures to deal with the symptoms of cardiovascular disease, but it is not so great at recognizing and preventing its root causes. Nevertheless, stress has now been accepted as a risk factor for cardiovascular disease.

It is ironic that a mere forty years ago, medical science rarely considered stress a factor in disease. Now its role is indisputable. We know that stress can be harmful even to our DNA. Our immune system, our brain, our cardiovascular system, and our DNA are all affected by stress. However, what is stressful is determined only in part by external circumstances. In a company of soldiers on the same battlefield, some will get PTSD, and some won't. It is the strength of their systems, which is heavily influenced by the quality of tending they received from gestation through childhood, that determines how they can handle the impacts they receive. Knowing this, how important it becomes to make healing the wounds of childhood and culture a top priority!

Dr. Elizabeth Blackburn, a Nobel Prize-winning scientist, opened a body of research involving telomeres. Telomeres are repetitive DNA sequences that protect the ends of chromosomes from fraying over time. In general, the older the individual, the shorter the telomeres. Shorter telomeres are associated with a raft of diseases in adults, from diabetes to dementia. In a fascinating study done in Romania, it was found that children who were raised in orphanages had shorter telomeres than children who were raised in foster homes. This study demonstrates that deprivation, an insidious form of stress, affects children right down to the molecular level.[5] Children need someone to be present with them and to attend to their emotional needs as well as their physical needs. Being in an orphanage is an extreme form of deprivation; however, not receiving attention, attunement, empathy, and other emotional nutrients is also deprivation, albeit in a milder form. It is one many adults have suffered. Future research will tell us how our telomeres are affected by lesser forms of deprivation.

The Autonomic Nervous System: A Key to Heart Disease

Our hearts are extremely sensitive to any need to increase our responsiveness. Whenever we are aroused, whether that arousal is pleasurable or stressful, the heart beats faster to provide the body with more oxygen and fuel such as glucose. Elevations in blood pressure help us deal with environmental challenges, even if those challenges are not emergencies. When properly balanced, the stress hormones adrenaline and cortisol provide and restore energy, but they are problematic when out of balance. However, the autonomic nervous system just may be the key to heart disease. Consider the words of two cardiologists from the Mayo Clinic.[6]

> *The status of the autonomic nervous system, although often ignored by clinicians, is a major determinant of cardiovascular health and prognosis. Excessive sympathetic stimulation and diminished vagal tone not only are markers of an unhealthy cardiovascular system, but also in part cause the adverse events. Chronic Sympathetic Hyperactivity increases the cardiovascular workload and hemodynamic stresses and predisposes to endothelial dysfunction, coronary spasm, left ventricular hypertrophy, and serious dysrhythmias.*

In the next chapter, we will understand even more about sympathetic hyperactivity; let me say now that it begins with a PFC that isn't well developed. This allows the limbic system to operate without adequate supervision, so the individual's ability to self-regulate is compromised. His amygdala is more apt to kick into fight/flight at a lower threshold. Minor thwarting turns into a major frustrating event. He may be chronically irritated or annoyed or frequently anxious or worried. And remember I am not describing just a small percentage of the population but probably at least half.

Love Is a Delicious Antidote to Stress

There are many ways to talk about love—erotic love, platonic love, fraternal love, and love as the presence of God. We can also understand love as an experience that occurs when two people are in sync, connected, generally maintaining eye contact, and feel the delight in their connection, however brief. These are precious and highly nourishing moments that are high-octane fuel for the development of the infant's brain. Adults also require regular doses of this emotional nutrient; unfortunately, too many adults don't even know of its existence. The analogy of vitamin deficiency is a good one, because such a deficiency can have not too obvious yet serious effects over time.

High levels of stress make attunement and these love moments almost impossible. To enter a connection like this requires slowing our system down enough to feel and to be present. The high-speed, high-stress lifestyle of our times is not conducive to love. There is a catch-22 here. We need attuned love to develop resilience and the capacity to receive love. The less we receive, the more we need and the harder it is to receive. The comprehension, practices, and disciplines in this book are aimed at reversing this cycle, helping us to slow down and become more available for love. Love is a delicious antidote to stress.

Notes

1. Kiecolt-Glaser, J., Garner, W., Speicher, C., Penn, G., and Glaser, R. (1984), "Psychosocial Modifiers of Immunocompetence in Medical Students." *Psychosomatic Medicine*, 46, 7.
2. Dura, J. R., Speicher, C. E., Trask, O. J., and Glaser, R. (1994), "Spousal Caregivers of Dementia Victims: Longitudinal Changes in Immunity and Health," *Psychosomatic Medicine*, 53, 345–362.
3. Cohen, S., Frank, E., Doyle, W. J., Skoner, D. P., Rabin, B. S., and Gwaltney, J. M. (1993), "Types of Stressors That Increase Susceptibility to the Common Cold in Healthy Adults." *Health Psych.* 17, 214–223.

4. Russek, L. G. and Schwartz, G. E. (1996), "Narrative Descriptions of Parental Love and Caring Predict Health Status in Midlife: A 35-Year Follow-Up of the Harvard Mastery Stress Study." *Alternative Therapies in Health and Medicine,* 2, 55–62.
5. *Nature: The International Weekly Journal of Science,* published online, http://www.nature.com/news/2011/110517/full/news.2011.298.html.
6. Curtis, B., and O'Keefe, J. (2002), "Autonomic Tone as a Cardiovascular Risk Factor: The Danger of Fight-Flight." *Mayo Clinic Proc.* 77, 45–54.

8

A New Model of Our Autonomic Nervous System

To understand and appreciate the role of stress on our well-being and the effects of the wounds of childhood and culture, it is essential to have a rudimentary understanding of the newest model of the autonomic nervous system (ANS). Understanding this system will be enormously helpful. Healing arts practitioners will also find it invaluable in their work with others. Let's look at the nervous system, then focus on the ANS.

The nervous system, as a whole, is composed of the central and peripheral nervous systems. The central system consists of the brain and the spinal cord. The peripheral system consists of the somatic and autonomic systems. The somatic system refers to the nerves that direct movements of the head, trunk, and extremities. Also, those that direct sensory information from the environment back to the spinal cord and motor command centers of the brain. It is sometimes referred to as the voluntary nervous system because it controls the movements of skeletal muscles.

The Autonomic Nervous System

The autonomic nervous system (ANS) is responsible for maintaining internal stability and responding to urgency. It mediates involuntary movements, such as heart rate and temperature control (although some can be brought under voluntary control with meditation or biofeedback). It is a key for communication among organs within the body, and it coordinates efforts to maintain stability within cells, tissues, and organs. The two main divisions of the ANS are the sympathetic system and parasympathetic system. Both are controlled by the hypothalamus. This tiny, peanut-sized structure plays a key function in both the ANS and the endocrine system. The *sympathetic* fibers leave the hypothalamus and run primarily along either side of the spine. From there, they travel out to the many organs and muscles of the body. The sympathetic system is associated with the fight/flight response because it prepares us to defend ourselves by either running or fighting. It is also responsible—along with adrenaline—for many of the feelings we associate with intense stress, such as pounding of the heart, sweating, and tensing of our muscles. However, when this emergency measure is evoked repeatedly throughout the day, or when it is never fully turned off, we have a situation of chronic anxiety in its many manifestations.

The *parasympathetic* system's function is to ensure that the body's priorities shift back to internal needs after external demands have been met. At the end of a scary roller-coaster ride, for example, the parasympathetic system returns the organism to a state of equipoise. We can laugh, remember the thrill, and go about our day. The parasympathetic system has done its job.

The fibers of the parasympathetic system are found mainly among the cranial nerves, a set of twelve nerves that send fibers to all the facial structures, the throat structures, and the heart and digestive organs. The vagus nerve is the principal nerve complex of the parasympathetic system. Until recently, it was thought that the two divisions, sympathetic and parasympathetic, were designed to work in what is known as a coupled-reciprocal relationship. Imagine two kids playing on a seesaw easily moving up and down. This is what is meant by a coupled-reciprocal relationship. However, the relationship between the two branches of the autonomic nervous system is a bit more complex and a lot more interesting.

The Polyvagal Theory: A New Understanding of the ANS[1]

Most texts describe the sympathetic system as the first to activate in response to an external demand. The organism is preparing to mobilize for an emergency. Energy leaves the digestive area and heads for the extremities, musculature tightens, and adrenaline pumps. We are revved and ready for action! Ideally this is not a response we want to kick in frequently throughout the day, nor is it a response to be maintained for long periods. Why, then, would it be the first response to environmental demand, as we have thought it to be for so long? As it turns out, it's not. A new model of the ANS indicates the first response to demand is mobilization in the parasympathetic side of the system. This model, developed by neuropsychologist Dr. Stephen Porges,[2] has powerful implications for healing. Although what follows may seem somewhat complex, I ask you to hang in there. This is as simple and clear an explanation of this model as I have come across. It is also important to deepen our understanding of how the whole human organism is involved in our wounding, more than just our minds or our emotions.

The primary nerve of the parasympathetic division of the ANS is called the vagus nerve. It is cranial nerve number X, and it exits from the medulla, part of the brain stem. The brain stem is the lowest area of the brain where the spinal cord transitions to the brain. In mammals, the vagus nerve has two distinct strands that exit from different areas in the medulla. One part is myelinated, meaning these nerves are covered with a kind of tissue that acts as insulation and allows for much faster transmission of an impulse along its fibers. This is the ventral vagal. It exits from the front or ventral part of the medulla and travels to the facial area, the larynx, the esophagus, the lungs, and the heart.

The other division of the vagus nerve is unmyelinated, and thus the transmission of impulses is slower. It is called the dorsal vagal and exits from the rear or rear part of the medulla. It travels primarily to the area below the diaphragm, the visceral region. Some fibers reach the heart, but it does not exert a major influence there.

Three Stages of ANS Development

This understanding views the ANS in an evolutionary context with three stages of development. The oldest or most primitive part of the ANS is the dorsal vagal. Its primary function is to foster digestion and, to some degree, to slow the heart. Behaviorally, the dorsal vagal is associated with immobilization behaviors. Reptiles, for example, have only a dorsal vagal, so when a reptile, like a lizard for example, is confronted with a novel stimulus or threat, its first response is to freeze. This action of freezing is mediated by the dorsal vagal. This is the first phylogenetic stage of the ANS. In other words, in the context of evolution, the dorsal vagal came first. If the dorsal vagal remains overregulated (stuck fully on), which is one consequence of high-impact traumatic events, it can immobilize our system indefinitely. This compromises the functions of the ANS and results in clinical symptoms.

The second phylogenetic stage is the development of the sympathetic division of the ANS, a system that exists in all mammals. As it prepares the organism to mobilize its resources in response to a strong environmental demand or threat, it inhibits the activity of the dorsal vagal's effect on the digestion process. Energy moves away from digestion and sex (which are not important in an emergency) and to the arms and legs. So besides this transfer of energy, the sympathetic system keeps the dorsal vagal in check. It keeps us from being immobilized by an experience as it prepares us to fight or run.

If we were to place ourselves in an absolute ready position to fight or run, we would immediately feel all the muscles involved in those two activities. Most of the big outer-layer musculature is involved, including the large muscles of the back, shoulders, arms, pelvis, and legs. The ability to sense and therefore to fully contract and relax those muscles is an absolute part of the fight/flight mechanism. To the degree that we have full access to those tissues and the ability to engage them, we have the subjective sense that we are capable of running or fighting. It does not mean we are athletic or super strong; it simply means that our consciousness must be connected to those tissues so we can function optimally.

Chronic tension, compression, constriction, and disconnection from those tissues reduce our sense of being able to fully engage the actions associated with the sympathetic nervous system (i.e., fight/flight). This is not an all-or-nothing situation. It is gradated. It is important we have some sense of being capable of fighting or running to survive. This is a biological imperative.

The Ventral Vagal

The third and most recent system to develop is the ventral vagal. It makes its appearance among the higher mammals. Its myelinated fibers allow for a rapid regulation of your heart's output, which in turn allows for engagement and disengagement with the environment, *without the engagement of your sympathetic system.* Its activation inhibits the activity of the sympathetic system and modulates sympathetic activity to allow for a return to equipoise after sympathetic arousal.

The ventral vagal functions as a brake; when released, it allows for increased cardiac output without the necessity of engaging the more intense sympathetic system. *The slow release of this vagal brake permits modulated responses to psychosocial demands.* When it is not functioning well, the fight/flight response is evoked in situations that may bewilder an onlooker; it may be hard to see the threat to which the individual is responding.

For example, a young woman approaches a young man at a party, a very innocuous situation. In this case, the young man gets anxious and starts sweating, his heart rate increases, and he starts looking for an easy exit. His vagal brake is not functioning well, so he finds it difficult to respond to a mild social demand. Instead, his sympathetic system is activated, and he has entered the domain of fight/flight. Had he gone into fight, he might have assumed an aggressive or sarcastic posture. Had he gone into flight, he might have withdrawn or become inappropriately intellectual, avoiding any contact. If his vagal break was adequately functioning, he would engage the attractive lady in pleasant conversation.

When high-intensity impact experiences—or shock traumas—occur, the organism freezes to some extent or other. The degree to which we are frozen compromises our capacity to protect ourselves, to fight or flee, to feel and deal, to adapt, and to engage in intimate relationships. The function of the sympathetic division is to mobilize the organism for emergencies. When a situation really calls for a rush of adrenaline and a readiness to fight or run, it is vital to our survival that our system is capable. However, to the degree that we are frozen, we will experience some helplessness, a feeling of not being able to defend ourselves, to take care of ourselves. It is a very uncomfortable feeling that often prevents people from engaging in anything that could trigger these feelings.

The Social Engagement System

Social engagement is the first line of defense against stress and an antidote to its deleterious effects. Because the ventral vagal complex[3] innervates throat, neck, and facial structures—all organs of interpersonal communication—we can say that the ventral vagal mediates interpersonal communication as well as self-soothing and calming behaviors. It is impossible to overestimate the importance of this to understanding stress, impacts, and insults.

If our brake is functioning poorly, we will feel at the mercy of internal and external forces that others seem to negotiate with ease. Why? Because in such instances, the sympathetic is the first level of response to engagement. Again, the vagal brake is meant to be the first level of response. If the mechanism, including the tissues involved, is doing its job, many social situations would not be perceived as threats. In our example, the young man would be able to respond appropriately to the presence of the woman, and his fight/flight response would not be called into action. When it is not functioning properly, we are left with many fewer options for response. We respond to minor psychosocial demands as if they were threats. Further, we will be interpersonally less available and responsive. Many conditions, impacts, and insults result in diminished functioning of the autonomic nervous system and its elegant way of providing what we need biologically to feel and deal in the world.

In recent years, many studies have documented that the experience of being loved and socially connected are primary antidotes to stress. As we have seen, individuals who perceive their parents as loving and their relationship with them as close showed significantly fewer chronic illnesses in adulthood than individuals who did not feel close to their parents or perceive them as loving. Repeatedly, the research is showing that people who are socially engaged and have close relationships tend to be healthier than those who aren't and don't. A compromised ventral vagal system may be just one of the physiological substrates that impede the experience of being loved and connected. Why?

Much human communication is transmitted nonverbally. Our tone of voice, facial expressions, body posture, movements, and energy all provide information that accompany the words we speak. The ventral vagal complex mediates these expressions. Nerves don't live in isolation but as part of a whole system with the tissues they mediate. When any of us have suffered serious impacts in life, the functioning of the ventral vagal complex, *along with all the structures they mediate,* are affected. The many muscles and connective tissues of our face and neck will not have their full expressive capacity. They will be restricted. Our range of expression, and therefore of communication, will be diminished. The capacity to connect will be abridged. Life will lose some of its sweetness. Further, many of us have been reared in an environment that allows only a very limited range of human expression. As children, the way we obey the injunctions against expression is to begin tightening our facial muscles. Over time, we lose the ability to engage those expressions. Our muscles simply don't know how to move in unfamiliar ways. No expression, or even a flat expression, becomes automatic and the mechanisms of which the expressions are a part—in this case, social engagement—are rendered less effective.

In summary, there is a phylogenetic—meaning in the development of species—hierarchical structure of responses to stress, impacts, and trauma. The most recent response to arrive—found only in human beings—is the ventral vagal system, a sophisticated and minute biological adjustment function that allows us to respond to low-level psychosocial demands in a modulated and stress-free fashion. We can say that this is a physiological substrate of our ability to feel and deal. Also, its activation inhibits the sympathetic system so that tranquility is restored when a threat has been removed, which also facilitates our ability to feel and deal. However, if for whatever reason the ventral vagal system is compromised, the next system "up" is the sympathetic. Then, it takes less time for the sympathetic to engage and longer for it to shut down. An individual may exhibit symptoms of poor impulse control or become easily aroused, displaying flares of anger and reactivity. Other examples of fight behaviors in humans include hostility, resentment, anger, sarcasm, irritation, and aggression. Flight behaviors include withdrawal, passivity, not engaging, and avoiding. The implications of how this affects our ability to self-regulate should be increasingly obvious.

What happens if the sympathetic division of the autonomic nervous system is overwhelmed? It would mean that the individual is not capable of either fighting or avoiding the danger successfully, as in a sudden car accident, a mugging, or a rape. The fight/flight mechanism doesn't get a chance to do its job. The only option left is to freeze.

In my youth, I froze. The system in my body that was designed to protect me was frequently assaulted. In this situation, as well as in other shock trauma situations, the dorsal vagal ascends. It becomes overregulated, and the result is shutdown, freeze, immobilization, and collapse. The inability to fight turns to rage; the inability to flee turns to terror. Neither can be successfully expressed, a profound feeling of helplessness results. This is an example of the sympathetic division being overwhelmed. It remains highly charged, but it is overshadowed by the dorsal vagal. It occurs in cases of extreme trauma—a life-threatening accident, war experiences, a severe assault, a history of childhood abuse, etc. There is no escape so we cannot employ the emergency mechanisms of fighting or running. My story is an example of a situation where an organism was frozen at a very deep level. Fight/flight was occurring, but it was dominated by a general freeze response. It is analogous to trying to drive a car with one foot fully on the gas pedal and one foot slammed onto the brake.

This is a description of an organism in shock, yet it is possible that, on the surface, the individual appears relatively normal. Under the radar though, the cells and tissues throughout the body contract and compress. The body feels less spacious or numb. These responses may be subtle, or they may be very intense. In my case, there was nothing subtle about it. The shock was intense. People walk around in a state of shock, and even when it is not subtle, they often don't know they are in shock. I didn't; it was normal for me.

A major symptom of shock is an emotional life that is extremely shallow, with no feeling of vitality and aliveness. There may be bursts of impulsive rage or anger or a chronic sense of dread or anxiety. And some things are just not present: warmth, love, a deep sense of connection to others or nature, and the ability to be transparent and self-disclosing. Additional consequences include not being able to feel your body; sensations are dulled and beg for intoxicants so they can come to life. There may be a chronic state of vigilance and arousal in terms of physiological markers, such as heart rate and blood pressure. There are various ways in which this condition manifests, but these are very common.

Dr. William C. Reeves was on a quest to find the cause of chronic fatigue syndrome. After years of research, he began to suspect that abuse and stress were contributors. It may be clearer now just how chronic stress—and living with the result of unresolved, unhealed wounds—can be at the root of such a disease. When the prefrontal cortex is not optimally developed and/or when the social engagement system is not optimally functioning, self-regulation becomes a huge challenge.

A healthy ventral vagal facilitates satisfying, contactful, engaging, warm, loving interpersonal relationships; a weak ventral vagal would underlie interpersonal challenges. People who are relationship challenged, people who are easily frustrated and slow to recover, people who are always mildly depressed or anxious, people who struggle with deep feelings of shame, guilt, or inadequacy—all are stressed.

We have moved from the prefrontal cortex to the limbic system, particularly the amygdala, to the autonomic nervous system, and to the muscles and tissues of the face, neck, and vicinity. Porges's model of the autonomic nervous system brings us closer to a robust comprehension of a body, mind, relational, and spiritual understanding of where, why, and how growth can occur.

Notes

1. Porges, Stephen, *The Polyvagal Theory: Neurophysiological Foundations of Emotions, Attachments, Communication and Self-Regulation*, W.W. Norton, 2011.
2. Ibid.
3. By ventral vagus complex, I am referring to cranial nerves III, the oculomotor; VII, the facial; IX, the glossopharyngeal; and X, the vagus (Nolte, *The Human Brain*, 1993). These nerves function as a subsystem.

Reflections on the Heart

> The best and most beautiful things in the
> world cannot be seen or even touched ...
> They must be felt with the heart.
> —Helen Keller

It is time to return our hearts to their rightful place—to the center of human intelligence. As a culture, we have taken one organ—the brain—and equated it with intelligence. We have built altars to our rational, logical, and analytic capacities and have, to our great peril, *ignored the wisdom of our heart.* We have gone to the moon, we have put gigabytes of memory in the tiniest of spaces, yet we haven't come close to learning to live in peace and harmony. We pollute our air, water, and soil. We destroy forests and species in the name of progress. Perhaps the single most illustrative and unfortunate consequence is that we reduce ourselves to "minds" that are carried around by our bodies. It's the equivalent of shutting off half the horsepower in your vehicle, or using one of an aircraft's two engines. Would you choose to fly in that plane? This is a powerful example of a cultural wound. We simply do not understand the effects of this ignorance, but we do pay the price.

There is a field of medical science called Neurocardiology; it is the study of the nervous system of the heart and its relationship to the brain and the autonomic nervous system (ANS). Two physicians, Drs. Armour and Ardelli, wrote a text asserting that the complexity of the heart's own nervous system qualified the heart for consideration as a "heart brain."[1] The heart has more links to the brain than any other organ and has over 40,000 sensory neurons. These neurons sense pressure changes as well as heart rate and detect circulating hormones and neurochemicals. They send this information to the brain. These incoming signals have a regulatory role over many of the ANS signals that flow from the brain to the organs of the body, including the heart. Again, the heart processes information independently of the brain and the nervous system, and then it interacts with them as well, as with other processing centers throughout the body.

We can think of the heart as the center of the primary fluid system. The vascular network, going from the heart to everywhere in the body, and returning to the heart, travels thousands of miles.[2] The only other organ whose tentacles reach everywhere in the body is the brain. This partnership is a key feature of human wholeness. When the activity of the brain is considered to be the mind, as well as the source of intelligence, while the heart is relegated to the function of an elegant pump, we have the kind of culture where wisdom has little hope of flourishing.

In his book *The Heart's Code,* Paul Pearsall tells a poignant, heart-wrenching story to illustrate the heart's capacity to "think and remember." He was speaking at a conference to a group of psychologists and psychiatrists when a psychiatrist rose and shared the following story. An eight-year-old patient of hers had received the heart of another little girl who had been murdered. She was brought to the psychiatrist by her mother because she had begun screaming at night in dreams, dreams in which she saw a killer. After a few sessions, the psychiatrist felt she could not deny the reality of this little girl's experience and, with her mother's consent, called the police. Using the description provided by the girl, the killer was identified as the donor's murderer, captured, and convicted. In that room, Pearsall says, there were few dry eyes.

To bring clarity, remember Dr. Mae-Wan Ho's statement.

> *Whenever people speak of "consciousness" they usually locate it in the brain, where ideas and intentions are supposed to flow, and which through the nervous system, is supposed to control the entire body. I have always found that odd, for like all Chinese people, I was brought up on the idea that thoughts emanate from the heart. I have come to the conclusion that a more accurate account is that consciousness is delocalized throughout the liquid crystalline continuum of the body (including the brain), rather than just being localized to our brain or to our heart.*[3]

Our heart is a sensing, feeling, communicating organ. It is a self-organizing, highly complex information center that continually sends messages to the brain. There are four channels of communication between the heart and the brain. The first three are neurological, biochemical by way of hormonal exchanges, and biomechanical by way of pressure waves. The fourth is electromagnetic. These four channels of communication and the complexity of the heart's nervous system attest to the intimate relationship between heart and brain.

The intelligence of the heart is a way of knowing. The heart has a spiritual intelligence—one of the nine types as we've previously discussed—with the capacity to understand sacred and profound truths that simply defy rational understanding. It brings clarity and recognition of what is important and what is not. For example, most religions have their origin stories. Our culture places these stories in *contrast* to the findings of science and evaluates them from a rational perspective. Origin stories are not meant to be memorized and understood as historical events. *They are meant to elevate the vibration of our consciousness.* Examined from a rational, empirical perspective, they can seem foolish. However, the heart can recognize fundamental spiritual truths within them, illuminating our consciousness, and allowing us to grasp our essential unity as human beings. These stories are spiritual forces, helping us to open our heart. The awakened heart can hear and see what the eyes cannot.

This level of understanding is transcendent and elusive. It has a felt-sense quality of knowing and tends to occur in meditative states. Awakening our heart means another way of living. It is not just about our personal happiness and comfort. It is not about feeling great when things are going our way and bemoaning our fate when they don't. It's about knowing that no matter the circumstances, no matter what the winds of life deposit on our shores, we can engage, participate, reflect, derive meaning, and become better people. It's about wanting our life to make a difference, to contribute, whether it's to our family, our community, our country, or our planet. It's about knowing we are all connected in ways we are only just beginning to recognize.

The goal of life is to make your heartbeat match the beat of the universe, to match your nature with Nature. (Joseph Campbell)

The human heart is the most responsive organ in our body. The quality of the rhythm of its beat changes in response to each moment-to-moment interaction with our environment. It is like a cellular conductor broadcasting its message to our every cell, and that broadcast affects our perception, feeling, cognition, and health. Beating approximately 100,000 times per day and 40 million times per year, it changes its rate and quality of beat in response to ever-changing environmental circumstances. Within one conversation, the heart shifts countless times to reflect the feeling, tone, and quality of the conversation. Not only does it change its beat, but it also broadcasts that change to every organ and cell in the body, especially the brain. If this is not intriguing enough, consider that this broadcast also reaches those in close proximity to us. I am saying that our own "vibes" affect us and others. How is this possible?

The answer takes us to examine heart rate variability. When we take our pulse and record seventy beats per minute, it's natural to assume that the time interval between each beat is constant throughout that minute. This is not so! There is a natural variability in the time interval between beats. I am not speaking here of pathological arrhythmias but of natural, beat-to-beat fluctuations. Not only does the interval change, but there is a qualitative variability in the time interval between heartbeats. Musicians listening to the beat of a drum hear the quality and pattern of the rhythm. The rhythms of our heartbeats and the patterns of time interval variability have qualities that we can analyze to determine the degree of their coherence.

Research done by an organization called HeartMath[4] has demonstrated that the heart's ever-present rhythmic field has a powerful influence on processes throughout the body, including human feelings. Brain rhythms naturally synchronize to the heart's rhythmic activity. For example, during sustained feelings of love or appreciation, blood pressure and respiratory rhythms, among other oscillatory systems, entrain to the heart's rhythm. Their rhythms are in sync.

On an objective level, the coherence of our heart rhythms refers to the quality of interplay between the two divisions of our autonomic nervous system: the sympathetic and parasympathetic. The quality of that interplay manifests as the quality of coherence in the variability of the heart rate. In this sense, coherence means a certain global order in the system, a certain connectedness among parts, a uniform, synchronized pattern. Each part is doing its thing in relation to the whole. This is another aspect of coherence within the human organism.

It is important to appreciate that high levels of coherence are accompanied by good, positive feelings. So often, people say that everything is fine when, in fact, they are feeling rushed, pressured, worried, anxious, cynical, resentful, bored, constricted, unappreciated, disconnected, unhappy, unloved, tense, or any other of many negative states. If such challenging states are on the mild side, we assume normality. However, even if these states are only mildly negative, they are reflecting a certain degree of incoherence in the patterns of heart rate variability and thus in the interplay between divisions of the autonomic nervous system.

When we experience sincere, genuine peace in our hearts—or appreciation, warmth, care, compassion, love, or any version of true, positive feeling—those feelings reflect a high degree of coherence that has profound and positive implications for our health and well-being. We experience flow, efficiency, and ease.

Of all the body's organs, the heart is the most powerful generator of electromagnetic energy in the human body, producing the largest rhythmic electromagnetic field. As measured by an electrocardiogram, this field can be detected anywhere on the surface of the body. The heart's electrical field is about sixty times greater in amplitude than the electrical activity generated in the brain. The magnetic field produced by the heart is more than five thousand times greater in strength than the field generated by the brain and can be detected at least several feet away from the body.[5]

Signals generated by the heart have the capacity to affect people around us. One person's heart signal, as measured by an electrocardiogram, can affect another's brain waves, as measured by an electroencephalogram. When people touch or are close to each other, one person's heart signal is registered in another's brain waves. Thus, the heart is both an organ of perception and feeling and an organ of transmission. Much communication between human beings is generated from heart to heart. The quality of being, the quality of feeling that we experience in the presence of another, is driven by heart-to-heart, electromagnetic communication. If the heart is hardened or walled off from our awareness as a result of impacts, insults, or maltreatment, we lose the capacity to feel each other's presence. This is a profound loss!

There is abundant literature describing how much communication takes place nonverbally between mother and infant. According to the literature, this communication is mediated mostly via the right brain of the mother to the right brain of the infant. This right-brain-to-right-brain communication provides the biochemical nourishment needed for the synaptic growth of the brain, particularly in the prefrontal cortex areas. Yet when you understand the electromagnetic strength of the heart and how connected it is to the brain, it is compelling to appreciate the heart as a primary organ of transmission and reception between mother and infant. It is a key partner with the right brain in this essential, formative communication.

Pearsall in his classic, *The Heart's Code*,[6] describes an experiment conducted by Russek and Schwartz that illustrates the energetic connection between hearts and between hearts and brains. Two people sat opposite one another in the same room with their eyes closed and not communicating in any way. Using a complex measurement process that included ECGs and EEGs for both people, they recorded the results. The preliminary results indicated three possible energetic connections.

First, it appeared that a person's heart energy transmits to his own brain. Second, it appeared that one person's heart seems to exchange energy with the other person's brain. Third, it appeared that one person's heart transmitted to the other person's heart. These results were also reported in studies by McCraty at the Institute of HeartMath. Research demonstrates that we are all connected heart to brain and heart to heart.

Vagal Brake and Coherent Heart Rate Variability

What is the relationship between a strong and flexible vagal brake and coherent heart rate variability? The body of work done by the folks at the Institute of HeartMath and the body of work done by Dr. Porges and his colleagues both involve the ANS and the heart. Each uses different models and does different research. The HeartMath people use a mathematical model that evaluates coherence of the rhythm of heart rate variability, and they study how that coherence can be increased by positive heart feelings. Porges describes the neuroanatomy of the ANS and the importance of the ventral vagal, or the vagal brake, in preventing sympathetic or fight/flight activation. His research employs a direct measure of vagal tone, which is the scientific name for the vagal brake.

Fight/flight feelings are not positive feelings. They result from a perceived threat to the integrity of our organism, and when these feelings don't lead to action, the coherence of heart rate variability decreases. The HeartMath group and Porges's followers employ different methods to improve the quality of human life and human feeling. Generally speaking, both groups' objectives are the same: growing positive feelings in the heart and improving the quality of our lives.

Forgiveness

> **Forgive us our trespasses, as we forgive those who trespass against us. (The Lord's Prayer)**

It seems inconceivable to write a book about healing the wounds of our childhood and our culture without considering forgiveness. In the process of awakening the heart and increasing its coherence, learning to let go of our hurts and forgiving perpetrators are essential. Even minor states of negativity decrease our heart rate variability's coherence. There is more noise in our system. To feel really open, appreciative, grateful, truly peaceful, and loving necessitates forgiving those whom we have perceived as hurtful in any way—including our parents and also ourselves. Holding on to resentments, rancor, and perceived injustices limits our heart's ability to live, love, and know. Holding on to resentments is like squeezing a sharp, flat rock and thinking we are hurting someone else.

As we begin to awaken our heart and develop our prefrontal cortex, it becomes easier to understand woundings in a different way. For example, for me, my crazy childhood provided my life's work; I have been able to be with many wounded people and empathize with their suffering and challenges. Further, I have been able to see my parents in the context of their history and understand how they were passing down what they received (or didn't receive). In other words, growing our comprehension facilitates forgiveness. My parents didn't wake up in the morning thinking about how best they could screw up their son's life. They were simply struggling to survive and cope with the very limited resources they had. I am in no way excusing their behavior; it was almost criminal. I am saying that my relationship to what they did has gone through quite a transformation.

To help our heart awaken and forgive, we need to be very firm with ourselves to not allow our thoughts to repetitively indulge our hurts and injustices. When someone has hurt us, we tend to continue replaying the event in our minds—or to replay what we have done wrong over and over again. Often, we need help to forgive. It could be from a friend, a therapist, a minister, or just from your relationship to the divine.

The Intelligence of the Heart

Intelligence is a function of the whole organism, and our heart, at its center, is as important as our brain. Here is an example of what I consider brain intelligence without heart. A recent *New York Times* article said that 17 percent of our Medicare budget is spent on the last six months of life. We consider death the enemy. How can that be? Only the inclusion of the heart can bring wisdom to this conversation, not only to save multibillions of dollars but also to make death a more positive experience for the elderly. Heart intelligence suggests that compassion and loving-kindness should be front and center in our lives—in our homes, in our businesses, and in our policies. The heart recognizes the essential unity of all humanity and seeks solutions that are inclusive. The heart sees the absurdity of dichotomies such as pro-life versus pro-choice and recognizes how both sides have important contributions to make to the conversation. The heart can hold the tension of opposites. The heart can say, "It is this *and* this."

Our heart knows that holding resentment, rancor, or hatred against any person or group is to inflict spiritual wounds upon ourselves (not to mention the injurious effects to our physical health). The heart can see the perfection in every moment in our life. Yes, I know without doubt that this wonderful moment I am experiencing as I write this page depended upon every moment that came before, and yes, that includes all my childhood. It is the heart that can hold both the hideousness of my childhood and the perfection of it. The analytic mind cannot grasp this and will dismiss it. Its comprehension is not sufficient.

Our heart recognizes that psychic phenomena exist and that "intuitives" can see and know in ways that boggle our conventional minds. In short, awakening of the heart to its place in the center of the organism, and as a key player in full partnership with the brain, leads to a much greater comprehension of the nature of life on earth.

What You Can Do: Practices

1. The quintessential practice to awaken and clear the heart is the practice of gratitude. Before sleep, or whenever you remember, take a few minutes to review your day and express thanks for all you have or have experienced. Don't overlook the small things: a neighbor's smile, your child's hug, the paper you completed, etc. And, of course, don't forget the not-so-small things: your partner's love, your good health, etc. But what if times are tough? Then the practice of gratitude is even more important. If you haven't noticed, negativity breeds negativity, and gratitude breeds more things to be grateful for.
2. Right up alongside gratitude in importance is the practice of appreciation. There is so much beauty in the world. Take a moment and let it in, whether it is a sunset, children playing, a rose, or a work of art. Pause, breathe, and absorb.
3. Think of someone or something you love unconditionally—a child, a pet, or a very special place in nature. Think of that person, pet, or thing while you also keep your attention on your heart. Notice the sensations and feelings around your heart. Cultivate those feelings.

For more practices on the heart, go to www.heartmath.com.

Notes

1. Armour and Ardelli, *NeuroCardiology,* 1994.
2. Google will say between 60,000 and 100,000. I had believed it was 25,000. Whichever it is, it's lots of miles.
3. Ho, Mae-Wan, *The Rainbow and the Worm: The Physics of Organisms,* World Scientific Publishing, 1998, p. 185.
4. See www.heartmath.com.
5. Ibid.
6. Pearsall, Paul. The Heart's Code. New York: Broadway Books, 1998, p.169.

10

Our Flesh Matters

Many human beings want to mend, heal, or improve from their childhood circumstances. However, few realize how those insults and impacts they received have affected them down to the level of their very tissues. We know our psyches are affected as well as our emotional life and even our relationships. We continue learning how our brain and nervous system are affected. However, we are just beginning to realize that our very tissues are affected as well.

Why I Didn't Die

My past caught up to me. On October 10, 2001, in a hotel in Albuquerque, I had a severe heart attack. The pain was intense. For approximately forty minutes, I could neither lie down nor straighten up. It was as severe as any pain I had ever experienced. The sweat poured off my forehead. The pain was in my solar plexus; I didn't experience any pain in my chest or arm, so I—in my infinite wisdom—assumed I had somehow yanked my esophagus out of my diaphragm and decided to sweat it out. Finally, the pain subsided and I went to bed. The next morning, I felt a general sense of malaise but no pain, so I went about my business for the next two days in Albuquerque.

The trip back to Seattle was excruciating, but once home, I felt fine again and managed to teach a workshop that weekend with no discomfort. Convinced of my hypothesis that the intermittent pain I felt in my solar plexus was GI, I attempted to modify and lighten my diet. When after a month I was still experiencing pain daily, but on a seemingly random basis, I went to my physician. In fairness to him, the way I framed my story led him to order x-rays of my abdominal area.

It was a slow process to schedule two rounds of appointments for x-rays and for receiving the results, which were all negative for a GI problem. In those three months, I went on three airplane trips and went snowshoeing in the mountains several times. Repeatedly, I would walk for a hundred yards or so and then had to stop until the pain subsided. Even so, I just couldn't imagine that anything was wrong with my heart. I was only fifty-nine years old and had been living a rather healthy lifestyle for over twenty years.

Finally, I was out of hypotheses and consulted a cardiologist. He said, "I don't think we'll find anything wrong with your heart. You look too healthy." He ordered an echocardiogram and then an angiogram. To my disbelief, he discovered that three major coronary arteries were almost entirely shut down and a blood clot was loitering in my left ventricle. Much of my left ventricle (that's the chamber that pumps blood to the whole body) looked like it might be gone (infarct, dead). With so little of my left ventricle functioning, it was astonishing that I was able to walk at all. My cardiologist, Dr. Jim, was incredulous. "I can't believe you walked in here. We call this pattern the 'widow-maker.' It kills men your age."

I had to wait a week to take a thallium scan to determine whether my left ventricle was mostly dead or just hibernating. It was a surrealistic week. There we were, praying for a triple bypass. The alternative was a transplant. At last, some good news: the thallium scan revealed that the ventricle was mostly hibernating, except for the apex. According to Dr. Jim, the apex of my heart was indeed infarct, never more to return to life. That was the good news!

When the clot dissolved, surgery was performed. Having had ample time to prepare—I recommend preparing for surgery whenever you have the opportunity—the procedure went gracefully. Three months later, after a second thallium scan, Dr. Jim called to say he needed another echo because the results of the scan suggested that the apex of my heart was no longer infarct, and he knew that couldn't be true. He was a very experienced and competent cardiologist; he just didn't make those kinds of errors, and everyone knows that cardiac tissue doesn't just regenerate.

"Impossible! I have never seen this in fifteen years of administering these tests," Dr. Jim's assistant confidently proclaimed just before turning on the echo. Five minutes later, he turned sheepishly to me, his demeanor visibly altered, and said, "Man, you should go to Las Vegas. You are one lucky dude."

The questions are these:

- How did I survive a serious heart attack for three months with no intervention?
- How did I present so well that the cardiologist predicted he wouldn't find anything wrong?
- How did I survive three round-trip flights and snowshoe trips with three of my coronary vessels almost completely closed and a blood clot in my ventricle, which itself was barely functioning?
- How did the apex of my heart, pronounced infarct by a competent cardiologist, return to normal?

I will offer three hypotheses, and you can choose the most likely. One, it was sheer luck. Weird things do happen. Two, it was divine intervention. It was not my time, and somebody up there liked me. Three, the level of organic coherence—fluidity, integration, and wholeness—I had attained over the years was sufficient to overcome the disorganization that manifested as the symptoms I described. Personally, I prefer hypotheses two and three. In considering the "good luck" hypothesis, add to what I mentioned above the fact that two days before my heart attack, we put an application for a new health insurance policy in the mail. As a result, the company covered my surgery.

I had already done a great deal of personal work, including years of various types of psychotherapy, many sessions of Hellerwork Structural Integration/Rolfing, years of practicing Continuum/yoga movement, and much more. There is no doubt in my mind that I would not have survived otherwise.

Realizing that my problems were not "just in my head" is what set the course of my entire adult and professional life. From 1964, when I first realized I needed help, until 1968, I assumed I needed psychological help only. This seemed an obvious conclusion considering that my challenges were in the domain of self-esteem, deep shame, relational incompetence, and so forth. My assumption wasn't entirely incorrect; I did need a great deal of psychological help. However, it was not until I directly engaged my neuromuscular and connective tissues through bodywork and movement that the more profound changes I was hoping for began to come about. What was it about my body that so cried for help? I was wound tight. I had very little breathing room. The lower part of my rib cage protruded and could never fully relax, meaning that my diaphragm could never let go to allow a full exhalation. My chest had a sunken look, as if I already was defeated by life.

Remember the vagal brake and heart rate variability. Consider that the exhalation phase of respiration utilizes the parasympathetic system, and if the diaphragm does not fully release with exhalation, it affects the quality of the vagal brake and our heart rate variability. In other words, the exhalation phase of respiration affects the moment-to-moment quality of how we feel. The sense of a deep, easy relaxation cannot really happen as long as our rib basket cannot fully release.

My neck also was one of the most affected areas of my body. The tension was chronic and unbelievable in its intensity. Consequently, I had difficulty feeling almost anything below my neck. I was quite literally cut off from myself. My eyes usually had a deeply pained look. My facial muscles were so taut that I conveyed little feeling in my face. I was tired almost all the time, and I had frequent migraine headaches. There was a profound disconnection between my consciousness and my body. Think of a cat moving stealthily toward a prey. Every motion seems to be intricately within the cat's awareness. This is what connection between consciousness and the body looks like. I was disconnected. I could not move fluidly, coherently. Even though it required a trained eye to see, the early years of abuse, beatings, and constant humiliation had had brutal effects on my body.

Today, in my eightieth year, I am significantly more fluid, spacious, connected, and integrated in my body than I was when I was forty. As a Continuum teacher, I teach fluid movement. Here I am, teaching my students, many of whom are in their thirties and forties, how to be and move fluidly in their bodies and lives. Of course, this pleases me, especially given where I began. However, there is an implication that is far more important. The average adult human body is far more constricted, compressed, and disconnected from consciousness than we can even imagine. What is "normal," in the sense of "This is how most of us are," is not even close to what is possible and perhaps to what is essential to our nature.

I was given a gift in being extremely dysfunctional psychophysically. I was compelled to search, to seek wholeness, and to keep from suffering daily. What we consider normal aging, normal living with its aches and pains, normal use of drugs—legal and otherwise—normal use of alcohol, normal eating, normal hundreds of billions spent on health care, and normal relating and loving—these are normal *in a statistical sense only*. What we have taken as normal is far removed from what is possible.

Ideally, our tissues ought to feel more like a wet sponge: yielding, elastic, fluid, supple, responsive, receptive, and vibrant.

Contrast this with a dry sponge. We have so much more room for feeling, sensation, nuance, and texture than we can even begin to imagine. All of this relates to our sense of well-being, to our health, to our aging process, to our capacity for deep intimate connection! The quality of our tissues is a significant aspect of our coherence, our wholeness.

Because this is clearly not something that is generally understood, let's look closely at what I mean by tissues. There are four types of tissues in the human body: muscle, epithelial, nerve, and connective. There are three types of muscle tissue: skeletal, smooth, and cardiac. *Skeletal muscle* is a voluntary type of muscle tissue that is used in the contraction of our bones. *Smooth muscle* is an involuntary type of muscle tissue found in the walls of internal organs and blood vessels. The *cardiac muscle* is involuntary in nature and is found only in the walls of our heart.

Epithelial tissue covers our body surface and forms the lining for most of our internal cavities. The epithelial tissue provides protection, secretion, absorption, and filtration. Our skin is an organ made up of epithelial tissue, and it shields the body from dirt, dust, bacteria, and harmful microbes.

Nerve tissue is composed of specialized cells that receive stimuli and conduct impulses to and from all parts of the body. Nerve tissue is found in the brain, in the central and peripheral nervous systems.

Connective tissue is the most abundant and the most widely distributed of the tissues. It ranges in density from bone, which is the hardest—although bone is approximately 15 to 20 percent water—all the way to blood. Yes, blood is considered a connective tissue. Most of the fluids in the body—blood, lymph, and cerebral spinal fluid—are considered connective tissue. The connective tissue we are most interested in here is called fascia.

Fascia is a fascinating tissue and forms a continuous web throughout the entire body. Very little was known about it until recently. Just about everything in the human body is covered in fascia. It is found superficially under the skin, acting as a body stocking over the entire body. It slips over every muscle. A skeletal muscle is made up of muscle bundles, and each bundle is covered by fascia. Each bundle is made up of muscle cells or fibers, and each muscle cell is wrapped in fascia. It covers every organ of the body. In the brain, fascia is known as *meninges*; in the heart, as the *pericardium*; over bones, as *periosteum.*

The fascia that wraps the muscle fibers and muscle bundles comes together at the end of the muscle in what we call a tendon. The tendon is not connected directly to the bone, as many believe; rather, it is connected to the periosteum, the fascia of the bone. In certain places on the body—for example, around the ankle joint—are bands of fascia know as *retinaculum.* In other places—across the top of the head, for example—are sheets of fascia known *aponeurosis.* Thus, ligaments, tendons, cartilage, superficial fascia, deep fascia, aponeurosis, septa, and retinaculum are all part of the continuous network throughout the entire body.

If it were possible to remove every other tissue and organ from the body and leave only the fascia, we would have a three-dimensional representation of our entire organism. The fascia forms a three-dimensional matrix of structural support, thus creating a unique environment for the functioning of our body systems.

To envision the relationship of fascia to muscle, picture an orange. If you peel an orange, the white that surrounds the orange represents the superficial fascia. If you quarter an orange, you will see that the white interpenetrates the quarters. If you look at still smaller pieces, you will see tiny slivers of white mingled with the orange. These represent each muscle fiber, covered in a layer of fascia.

Fascia is comprised of three components: *collagen,* which is the toughest of the three and is the supporting component (within the collagen protein is an ordered network of water molecules), *elastin,* which is tissue that is elastic, and an *amorphous ground substance,* which is gelatinous. It transports metabolic material through the body and acts like a cushion. Fascia is very moist.

Fascia forms a unitary matrix so if we could take hold of it in some way and give it a little twist, the ramifications would resonate throughout the organism. To visualize this concept, think of a lovely, special sweater that fits you perfectly. Now imagine a snag or pull in the material of the sweater. The effects can gradually create a change in the entire sweater, causing it to lose its shape and integrity. It would no longer fit in the same way. This is what happens with fascia. It is, indeed, a tissue that is present throughout our body and is affected by the events of our life, from conception to the present.

Fascia and Communication

Water layers on the collagen fibers provide conduction pathways for rapid intercommunication throughout the body, enabling our organism to function as a coherent whole. Collagen is the principal protein; it makes up approximately 70 percent of all the proteins in connective tissues. The picture that emerges is of a vast network of high-speed processing that is taking place in the connective tissue system. Water is the critical element in this high-speed, instantaneous communication and coordination of the human body, and water is what allows for coherent functioning.

Another factor that supports this intercommunication is the patterned nature of collagen. According to Mae-Wan Ho,[1]

> *Patterns of collagen fiber alignment are important for biological organization and function. These patterns affect not only the mechanical properties of the connective tissues, but, through the network of associated structured water, also the electrical conductivity and detailed circuitry for intercommunication, on which the health and well-being of the individual depends.*

No longer does science believe that connective tissue serves only as a mechanical supporting function. This new narrative has not yet become part of mainstream science, but the science is there, and what we see is how communication is a big part of the functions of connective tissue. To sum it up and quote Dr. Ho one more time:

> *Quantum coherence is possible because of the 70 percent or so of water that makes up an organism. Quantum jazz is the music of the organism dancing life into being. It is played out by the whole organism, in every nerve and sinew, every muscle, every single cell, molecule, atom, and elementary particle ... Intercommunication is the key to quantum jazz. It is done to such sublime perfection that each molecule is effectively intercommunicating with every other, so each is as much in control as it is sensitive and responsive. And intercommunication is predominantly electronic and electromagnetic, thanks to liquid crystalline water ...*[2]

So when I say that our tissues ought to feel somewhat like a wet sponge—yielding, elastic, fluid, supple, responsive, receptive, and vibrant—I am referring not only to our muscles but to our connective tissues as well. In fact, the two are impossible to separate. It is my belief that our fluid nature is what allows us human beings to resonate with each other. Our fluid nature is what allows us to experience exquisite connections that we can call love. Water is a highly resonant substance, and our hearts are at the center of our fluid system, so I believe it is our hearts and our fluidity that most allow for our ability to be in close harmony with one another.

From Tissues to Structure

Our body is a physical structure, and as such, it obeys the laws of physics and architecture. The major structural components of the human body should be—ideally—in alignment with each other. Misalignments, such as the head jutting forward, twists, or displacements—have consequences, and those consequences are not merely physical. Why? Because coherence means that every aspect is influencing and being influenced by every other.

Movement

The quality of our tissues and the quality of our structure are reflected in how we move. We can think of movement in two ways. One is functional: how we sit, stand, walk, bend, reach, or lie down. The other is how our tissues move. For example, how do our tissues move when we breathe? How responsive, receptive, fluid, and elastic are they? Both kinds of movement are important. For a thorough understanding of functional movement, see the works of Judith Aston,[3] Mary Bond,[4] or Dan Bienenfeld.[5]

Our childhood and cultural wounds affect the entire organism. Our entire organism must be addressed in the process of healing—*body, mind, spirit, and relationships.* We can no longer afford to overlook our body structure—its muscular system, connective tissue, and fluid systems. It is fabulous that scientists have included the brain and even the autonomic nervous system in their areas of investigation. Let's not stop there. There is another whole universe to explore.

What You Can Do: Practices

- Practice accepting your body. This practice is vital and extremely challenging. A hundred "Yes, buts" may come up, but just let them come and let them go. Yes, of course, you may prefer a smaller waistline or stronger arms or whatever, but accept your body exactly as it is. I have worked with hundreds of individuals over the years, and the percentage of people who like their bodies is very small, especially women. Our culture tortures women with unrealistic and unhealthy ideals. Realize that judging and criticizing your body will not change a thing. What it will do is make you disconnect further from your body. Doing something like moving, exercising, changing your eating patterns, or receiving bodywork is what will help. But the absolute best place to change anything is from a place of acceptance. Further, disliking an area of your body results in greater disconnection from that area.

- Listen to your body. Learn to pay attention to your heart and to your guts. Learn to feel your legs and arms. You can easily incorporate body awareness into your walks. As you walk, let your awareness sense the movement of your arms and legs. Walk as if your mind were located inside your body. You can select areas, such as your arms and legs, or you can tune into your back for a while. Certainly, tune into your breath. Sense your breath as you walk. I have been doing this practice for decades, and I still find new ways and places to tune into.
- Practice softening your belly. A hard belly is a first-line defense against soft, tender feelings. It signals a decrease in coherence. Whenever you remember, allow your belly to soften as much as it can.
- There are many different breath exercises to practice. One is the three-part breath. Take an easy breath, sensing a front-to-back movement between your pubic bone and your coccyx (i.e., from very low in your belly to the lowest part of your back). As your soft, easy breath continues, feel the lower part of your ribs expand laterally and widen. And finally, feel the very top of your ribs and clavicles expanding

from front to back. Many people tend to breathe high in their chests and find it difficult to feel any movement low in their bellies. Others breathe very low but can get almost no movement in their chests. Ideally, you should be able to feel all your tissues as they respond to your breath everywhere, including in your arms and legs.

There is no one right way to breathe. Breathing is contextual. Different breathing is required in different situations. You breathe differently when you run than when you watch television or make love. But as your body becomes less and less constricted, as you breathe, you will be able to feel an easy movement in three places: low in your belly and in your lower back, in the lower part of your ribs all the way around, and at the top of your ribs and clavicles.

Notes

1. Ho, Mae-Wan, *The Rainbow and the Worm: The Physics of Organisms,* World Scientific Publishing, 1998, p. 190.
2. Ho, Mae-Wan, *Living Rainbow H2O,* World Scientific Publishing, pp. 4–5.
3. Aston, Judith, *Going beyond Posture,* www.astonkinetics.com.
4. Bond, Mary, *The New Rules of Posture: How to Sit, Stand and Move in the Modern World,* Healing Arts Press, 2006.
5. Bienenfeld, Dan, *Align for Life* (e-book), www.danbienenfeld.com.

Introduction to Part 2

The Journey

Over the past fifty-plus years, I have immersed myself in education and training programs in different approaches to psychotherapy, somatic therapy, and structural bodywork. It's been quite an education and bestows on me a modicum of credibility to discuss the healing journey. However, my fifty-five years as a student, a client, and a seeker in search of healing have most qualified me for this task. It has been my personal adventure, and as with all great adventures, there have been times it has felt arduous, at times exhilarating, at times quite ordinary. Yet the value and rewards have been immeasurable. Simply stated, I am a different organism from what I was when I began. As I write this, I know I have not even come close to the end of the trail.

We have seen how there are three major areas where we have likely been wounded: our identity, our connections, and our personal sense of responsibility, meaning our sense of being the authors of our life. We have seen how these wounds occur and how we are affected by them.

Now it is time to examine the opportunities we have to evolve and enrich our lives. The essential first step is to recognize how much more life can offer and how limiting are the offerings of conventional culture. Many of us assume life is about successfully reaching certain milestones and managing day to day to the best of our ability. For too many of us the gospel is to get a good education so you can have a good career—or at least a good job. Then find a partner with whom to raise children. Save and invest wisely to be financially secure. Enjoy holiday meals together with your extended family. These are all good things. But they are only the beginning. Seeing them as the ultimate in life's sweetness is in and of itself part of the problem.

Throughout history, the great thinkers have beseeched us to examine ourselves, to wake up, and to learn and grow. From Pythagoras to Socrates, from Buddha to Jesus, we're told there is so much more. It is now, in this twenty-first century, that the concepts and practices have become more and more available to us all.

In the following chapters, we will consider four interrelated areas of being. None can be ignored if we are to fully embrace this journey of evolution. They are the somatic, the emotional/psychological, the relational, and the spiritual.

In chapter 11, we begin with the somatic. Obviously, we are all familiar with "the body," but less familiar with the understanding that our connection to our feeling sense of our body is not the same as the body as an object, as a thing. In other words, there are two dimensions to the body: one is the body itself—organs, joints, systems, etc. The other dimension, much less studied, understood, or appreciated, is our feeling connection to our body, our experiencing our body.

In chapter 12, we will begin with somatic psychotherapies and then move into psychotherapies, especially those I consider to be highly valuable for all of us. These include AEDP (accelerated, experiential dynamic psychotherapy)* and voice dialogue (from the Jungian-based psychology of selves). We will also include some of the available seminars that can offer much in support of this journey.

In chapter 13, we will explore the relational dimension. The committed intimate relationship is a gold mine of possibilities for

* The dynamic in AEDP refers to psychodynamic, which refers to the long lineage begun by Freud.

joy, learning, and self-discovery. It's an area of unparalleled richness in which we can continue to grow throughout our lifetime.

We will complete this story in chapter 14 with the spiritual dimension of our existence. To consider human growth and development while ignoring the spiritual is as egregious as ignoring the body in attempting to understand our wholeness. I will share my experience of being a disciple on a path whose sacrament is generically known as ayahuasca. Sacred substances have been part of spiritual traditions for centuries and offer a unique resource in the process of illumination. Illumination is the true objective of spiritual development.

11

The Somatic Dimension of Wholeness

Entering the somatic dimension of healing may for most readers be a new way to look at becoming whole. The idea that the body is somehow related to emotional healing or spiritual development has been around for a long time. One common notion we've seen is the body is the temple of the spirit; therefore, we must take care of the body. Another notion is that we store emotions in different places in the body and these must be released for us to be free and whole. There is truth to this idea; however, it is only a small part of how the body relates to our experience of ourselves and the world. Let's say we want to develop more confidence, more capacity to speak from our hearts, more capacity for emotional intimacy, more assertiveness, more tenderness, more feeling, and more capacity to express our love and to receive love; all of these involve the body. However, it is not the body as we normally think about the body. It is not getting the body to "behave" in a different way. *It is the feeling sense of the body that must be awakened and evolved.* It is our inhabiting our body with consciousness, energy, vitality, life force, and growing presence.

A simple example. If there is a vibrant, alive sense of our legs, then we are more likely to feel a secure sense of being related to the ground, an inner sense of groundedness. If one's shoulders are raised high toward the ears and the pelvic floor is also pulled up, it is challenging at best to feel safe because the body is locked into a fear position. Another example. Gut feelings are difficult to have if the individual is not present in his guts and sensation is limited. One more example. Our back muscles are some of the strongest muscles in our body. The muscles and fascia of our back connect directly to our arms. However, if we don't sense this connection, if it is not part of our feeling sense of our body, then our sense of ourselves will be weaker than it could be if this sensory connection were present. I am postulating that *the foundational effect of every trauma, in addition to whatever other neurological or psychological effects it may have, is a loss of a feeling sense of our body.*

There are two general ways the feeling sense of our body is diminished. One is through impacts of all sizes and scopes that affect our tissues. When muscles become chronically tense, when connective tissues lose their fluidity, when tissues become dense, compacted, or contracted, our ability to feel them, their relationships, and psychosomatic functions such as groundedness, diminish. Again, we're talking about sense of self.

The second general way we reduce our sense of wholeness, our feeling sense of our whole body, is through life-negating injunctions—cultural, familial, or religious. If, for example, I am reared in a generally congenial, caring home, but one that implicitly affirms that sex is not to be part of my experience, I will obey the injunction by not inhabiting and feeling my pelvis.

How we comprehend our body and its needs goes a long way in determining how we care for ourselves. In the late 1940s and early '50s, few knew how our actions and lifestyles were related to our health. Most people smoked and gyms were virtually unknown. As the '50s progressed, the idea of the importance of not being sedentary began to appear. Also in the '50s, the idea that nutrition was important to our health began to emerge, even though to this day agreement on what constitutes good nutrition is hard to find.

A consensus has evolved that adequate nutrition and ample exercise are the primary components of good self-care. More recently, stress-management has been added, yet as we have seen, our culture's understanding of stress management is still in its infancy.

In my personal experience and research, there are three things most of us are just beginning to learn and appreciate about our body. *First,* our connection to, and the quality of, our subjective experience of our body is vitally important. It's "the body" from the inside, our sensing/feeling body. The *second* thing that most don't know is that through a variety of movement practices, our body has the potential to help us expand our very sense of who we are. The *third* thing we are beginning to understand is the architecture of our body is also highly significant. The idea of balance of muscle groups and structural alignment has been with us for decades; however, the vast majority of our population has yet to learn the importance of this concept.

The Somatic Perspective—Our Body from the Inside

When we look at a human body from the outside, whether he is walking, sitting, or lying on an operating table, what we see is a body. Anatomists, physiologists, physicians, and artists have studied the human body extensively for centuries. The data they have accumulated is impressive and has benefited humankind enormously. However, it is not complete, nor can it ever be complete until we recognize that we are observing our organism from just one side: the outside looking in.

Now let's consider our body from the perspective of our experience. The distinction between the body as a third person object (an "it") and the body as a first person (I) was most clearly articulated by Dr. Thomas L. Hanna.[1] At the heart of Tom's theory is the critical importance of awakening the whole sensing-feeling body. This is perhaps Thomas Hanna's most important contribution to the field of human understanding. In order to comprehend this crucial distinction between being outside and looking in, and feeling from the inside, he chose the term *soma* to name the living body *as it is experienced.*

Soma, from the Greek for "living body," refers to sensations, feelings, movements, and intentions. Hanna was emphatic that any attempt to understand the human being without understanding this somatic view must be incomplete. Science and medicine, committed to its third-person, objective view, are doomed to suffer inadequate and insufficient results. The human body must also be studied *from the inside.* This is the somatic perspective. Hanna said,

> *The great calamity of the human sciences is that we have, as it were, ganged up on ourselves. Only one person can see himself or herself as a first-person somatic being, but millions of people can see that person as a third-person bodily being. Consequently, these millions can join together and observe, measure, and diagram the objective body of the human person. That is the easy and obvious way taken by sciences.*[2]

But what is obvious and easy is not always complete and effective. For Tom Hanna, how we age is the most obvious consequence of the gross neglect of the first-person, "I" side of our body. He challenges the assumptions that it's normal to lose mobility, become increasingly more rigid, and become beset with aches and pains. We can study the third-person body forever, but until we include the somatic perspective, we will miss the mark because we will miss the condition that underlies the majority of problems associated with aging.

He called this underlying condition *sensory-motor amnesia (SMA)*. Optimally, skeletal muscles operate under the control of the cerebral cortex, which means they're under voluntary control and can be contracted or relaxed at will. Sensory motor amnesia is the loss of voluntary control of our musculature, which results in chronic tension. It means not being able to fully contract or fully relax a given muscle. This is not just a physical issue, even though if it somehow were only that it would still be quite serious. It's important to know that wherever we have lost those connections (i.e., where sensory-motor amnesia has set in), *we are suffering a deficit in our sense of self.* For example, if we can't clearly sense the powerful muscles of our back and pelvis, we will likely not feel as powerful as we actually are. How does SMA occur?

As we have seen, the brain can be viewed as having three major parts: the reptilian brain, the midbrain or limbic system, and the cerebral cortex. Ideally, the cerebral cortex has control of our 640 skeletal muscles. However, as a result of impacts and insults, sustained stress, abuse, speed, etc., the locus of control of many muscles shifts from the higher cortex to the lower centers of the brain. Once this happens, we cannot consciously intend these muscles to relax, because the cortex isn't receiving the sensory input necessary for relaxation to occur. Muscle action occurs in a feedback loop between sensory and motor neurons. Without the sensory input, the cortex loses control and muscles remain contracted. Recall how chronic tension serves as a feedback loop to the limbic system, maintaining it in a state of hypersensitivity. This means that it sets off the fight/flight response at a lower threshold or is unable to turn it off, which is another negative consequence of what Hanna called sensory-motor amnesia or chronic tension. Further, because this happens gradually over time, we don't realize we have lost this ability. We simply feel normal; this is who and how we are.

Based on his clinical work and understanding of neurophysiology, Hanna described two basic reflexes that organize patterns of muscle tension: the *red-light reflex* and the *green-light reflex*. He calls the accumulative effects of these two reflexes the *senile vise grip,* suggesting that the way we age is a result of these patterns.

The *red-light reflex* is a startle or withdrawal response. For example, if we are walking down the street and suddenly hear a loud explosion or the sound of gunfire, in milliseconds, our body will move into a protective posture. Our jaw muscles will contract, followed immediately by the muscles around our eyes and brow. Our shoulder muscles contract, elevating our shoulders as our head juts forward. Our abdominal muscles contract, bringing our chest down and our head farther forward as our diaphragm contracts, obstructing our breathing. Our pelvic floor tightens, and our knees point inward as our ankles roll inward. All of this occurs in a moment of being severely startled.

Obviously, just as the stress response is adaptive and necessary for survival, this reflexive action is a means of protection. When our muscles can relax and return to their normal state after the danger passes, there is no problem. However, when this reflex becomes habitual, for example, when a child is frightened repeatedly, the muscles cannot return to a relaxed state and sensory-motor amnesia sets in.

We have throughout this book discussed the effects of wounds of childhood and culture. There is one more that we have not given sufficient attention that fits best in the context of Dr. Hanna's work. It is the wound of excessive speed. The *green-light reflex* is another way through which tension accumulates and coherence diminishes. The green-light reflex is the opposite of the red-light reflex. Hanna sees it as a consequence of modern living in which we are guided by alarm clocks, schedules, calendars, quotas, coffee, and deadlines. It is the tendency in our culture to live in overdrive. Essentially, the green-light reflex is a "Let's go!" reflex; it contracts the large extensor muscles of the back. Whereas the red-light reflex is protective and curls the body forward, the green-light reflex is assertive and prods us to "go." The extensors of the back contract, the chest lifts forward, and the shoulders pull back. Both sets of movements are adaptive and essential, but when habituated, they cause sensory motor amnesia and its ensuing problems. Individuals who have suffered a great deal of fear tend to have a red-light reflex posture, whereas individuals who are assertive and "out there" tend to have a green-light reflex posture.

Our cultural emphasis on production, growth, and achievement is another aspect of the soil that brings toxic nourishment to our body. It goes against nature to expect constant growth, constant expansion. Nature has cycles of production and rest. Winter is arriving as I write. Leaves have fallen; flowers have left. It's a time of rest, consolidation, and renewal so that in the spring all will bloom again. Far too many Americans simply don't get sufficient rest, sufficient sleep. The sympathetic division of the autonomic nervous system is always in gear. Alcohol, drugs, and meds are the compensating factors for the inability to turn the system down.

In aging, most people reveal a combination of both red-light and green-light reflexes. Tom called this the *senile vise grip*. The fear and withdrawal reflex *and* the "Let's go" reflex are revealed in rotations and distortions of posture. Both are present, and we call the results "the challenges of aging." Most of us do not grow old in an agile, vibrant body. The forward-thrust heads, the elevated or pulled-back shoulders, the sunken or pushed out chests, the ribs compressed into the pelvis, the dense, rigid legs, the very tight backs with exaggerated lumbar curves or flattened lower backs with no lumbar curves—all broadcast habituated reflexes and announce the accumulated effects of our wounding, of living in overdrive, chronic stress, and poor movement habits. When our muscles cannot fully contract and relax, we cannot reach our full potential. We will not age with grace and fluidity. The solution is somatic education.

Hanna Somatic Education brings consciousness to our muscles and frees our movements. Based initially on the work of Moshe Feldenkrais, Hanna created a clinical-educational approach to help people who are in pain and teach people to live with more freedom. The field of Somatics has developed over the last half century through a process of inquiry into how consciousness inhabits the living body. Today, the field of somatic education has a growing international organization called the International Somatic Movement Education and Therapy Association (or ISMETA), which includes a wide variety of somatic disciplines.

If we want to get the most from the journey to healing, we should find classes or practitioners of the Feldenkrais modality, the Hanna Somatic Education, or any of the many others. In the past decade or two, yoga has become very popular, and for good reason. There are many benefits to be gained from yoga, but an understanding of what I am writing in this chapter will better prepare the student to harvest the goodies. A focus on striving to do the postures right will diminish the rewards. Instead, focus on feeling sensations, quality of breathing, and melting at the end of the stretch. These will make your practice a somatic education experience.

The second thing most of us don't know about our body is how it has the potential through various movement practices to transport us to profound emotional and spiritual experiences. Normally, we think of our body as bound and limited by our skin. Yet under certain conditions, as we will see later in this chapter, we can feel a sense of the dissolution of those boundaries and a sense of deep relationship to the space and people around us. Further, we know that the body is about 70 percent water and that from the perspective of physics, it's about 98 percent space. This is common, objective knowledge; what's not so common is the tremendous value of experiencing ourselves as vibrant, fluid, or spacious. Our internal experience of our body needs as much attention and education as we give to cardio or building muscles.

To Become Like Water Is to Become Your Self: Emilie Conrad and Continuum—A Movement/Meditation

---

Nothing in the world is as soft and as yielding as water. Yet for dissolving the hard and inflexible, nothing can surpass it. The soft overcomes the hard; the gentle overcomes the rigid. (Lao Tzu)

Of all the somatic disciplines and practices I have encountered, none has affected me as deeply as Continuum. Even one weekend workshop can change how we live in our body. As one student put it, "I don't have to sit still and be bored in meetings anymore." The practice of Continuum over time, especially if experienced in weeklong residential settings, has the power to result in moments of "oneness" that mystics write about. There can be a sense of dissolution of the egoic, bounded self; for me, these are moments of awe. Further, there are the possibilities of viscerally experiencing oneself as a continuity of our phylogenetic process. For example, I can move "as if" I am a reptile, but I can also experience "I am" the reptile, not as a thought, not as an image, but as a clear sense of self in the moment. This is a highly advanced level of practice, but it can be reached. I have had several moments of both types of experiences. These are identity-expanding experiences that are nourishing to the human soul.

The year was 1983. Never in my life had I seen such fluidity of movement. At the time, Susan Harper[3] was the only other person authorized by Emilie Conrad to teach Continuum: a movement/meditation. The way she moved seemed outside the range of what human beings can do. Her spine moved in waves and with apparently total freedom throughout all the many joints of her vertebrae. But her back movement wasn't only at the joints. What truly amazed me was the movement of the tissue under her skin. I felt like a complete klutz. How did anyone connect so deeply with themselves as to get the tissues to move like that? It was more than I could conceive. It would be many years before I began my study of Continuum in earnest.

From 1995, I have considered Continuum one of my meditation and movement practices. There is evidence in the literature that mindfulness practices can grow structures in the brain. Continuum is a mindfulness practice that can enhance not only our brain but also tissues throughout our body. Given what we have learned about water, it is not far-fetched to believe that the quality of the water in our cells and tissues influences our vibrancy, our vitality, and our sense of aliveness. As I see it, the quality of fluids in our bodies correlates with the quality of our tissues, cells, fibers, muscles, connective tissue, and so forth. In turn, the quality of our tissues correlates with the quality of our structure—and how the major components of our structure relate to one another. Each level influences and is influenced by every other level. Mae-Wan Ho tells us this is how it is at the subatomic and molecular levels and both macroscopically and microscopically.

> *The ideal coherent whole, I suggest, is also the ideal of health. The coherent organism is a unity of brain and body, heart and mind, an undivided bundle of intellect and passion, flesh, blood, and sinew that lives life to the full, freely and spontaneously, attuned not just to the immediate environment, but the universe at large.*[4]

Clearly this relates both to our body and the feeling sense of our body, the feeling sense of wholeness.

For almost fifty years, Emilie Conrad, the founder and primary developer of Continuum (along for many years with Susan Harper), said that the key to health and well-being lies in our body's water.[5] Further, through the use of sounds, mindful attention, and extremely slow and subtle movements, we can learn to participate with the fluid level of the body's movement. It was Emilie who developed a movement path that addresses the organism as muscle, as fascia, as sensation and feeling, as expression, *and as fluid.*

Every now and again a visionary sees a truth so simple yet so profound that it will generate waves of change for decades, if not centuries, to come. Conrad's contribution is the understanding that we are all connected to the fluid system of the planet on which we live. By fluid system, she is referring to the 326 cubic miles of water that bathe this planet—the water of the oceans, lakes, and rivers. She is referring to the water of the clouds that nourishes our trees and plants. She is referring to the water in our bodies, the blood and lymph, and the tears and interstitial fluids—the 70 to 80 percent water that I have been referring to. She is saying all that fluid comprises one continuous system. Not only are we part of this fluid sphere, but our connection to this biosphere is a primary source of nourishment analogous to our umbilical connection before birth. *We can be nourished by life itself. To the degree that our bodies are sufficiently open, sufficiently fluid, and sufficiently coherent, life itself is a source of nourishment.* It is a primary connection that renders us just a little less dependent on other sources of nourishment. The fluid system is the medium through which we are connected to the web of life—not as a concept but as a living reality. Seen through the lenses of conventional biology and chemistry, these assertions may appear outlandish. However, after looking at Mae-Wan Ho's work, Emilie's words seem prophetic. The wounds of life—as well as an insufficient comprehension of who we are in these bodies and what we need—have many serious consequences. *Among them is the severance of this connection to the universal nourishment that continually offers the possibility for delight at being alive in these bodies.* Children can feel supreme delight just running around the living room or jumping on a welcoming lap. They need so little to feel delight and joy. If reared in a relatively safe environment, and if their needs have been reasonably met, young children are still fluid and supple in their tissues.

Water, like children, loves to move. When water is forced to move along a straight path, it gives away energy. Water prefers waves, spirals, swirls, and spins. When water encounters an obstacle, its forward movement is stopped and it curls inward, forming a spiral. In this way, it gathers energy. The vortices in water interact with each other, and water always arrives at its destination with more energy than when it started out.[6] In this way, water is a teacher in Continuum as the student learns to move in tiny, subtle spirals, and small and large waves. Everything in our body—every organ, muscle, and cell—is surrounded by water and to some extent comprised of water. Become like water, and you become yourself.

Let's go directly to some words by Emilie Conrad.

> *Technically speaking, our bodies are not exactly ours. What we call a body is an open-ended expression of an ongoing universal process that is in constant flux, arranging, re-arranging, and experimenting as new formations come into existence. The continuum of life on land takes place with the galaxy and humans alike ... The fluid presence in our bodies is our fundamental environment;* ***we are the moving water brought to land ...*** *When we see a newborn, essentially, we are looking at the movement of water made flesh ... We are seeing a fluid system meeting the electromagnetic field of the earth, where an elegant exchange begins to take place.*[7]

Water carries the vibration of everything that is placed in it.[8] It is the ultimate example of receptivity. Water is perhaps the most resilient, adaptable substance on the planet. It can harden into ice and disappear into vapor. It is strong enough to gradually dissolve rock. In fact, each drop of rain forms an almost perfect sphere whose surface tension is strong enough to blast microscopic bits out of any landscape. It is an essential substance. Also, water absorbs energy from light and converts it to different types of energy, such as optical, electrical, mechanical, and chemical energy.

Water is the medium between heaven and earth. Water is transparent to light and is energized by light.[9] When you become like water, you become transparent, adaptable, resilient, and strong. You become receptive, and being receptive means you can allow love in. This is what I mean when I say that to become like water is to become yourself—your true self.

If water is the means, medium, and message of Continuum, the octopus is its best representative here on earth. To get a real feeling for what a student of Continuum is striving for, watch a video of an octopus. Its shape-shifting adaptability, strength, and fluidity are what every serious student of Continuum strives to emulate.

We have seen how the wounds of life affect our psyche, how they shape what we believe to be true about ourselves and others, and how they affect our brain, our nervous system, our physical structure, and the muscles, fascia, and fluids of our body. Repeatedly, I have argued that it is the organism as a whole that must be understood and addressed. Given that we are so highly fluid, it makes simple sense that an approach that recognizes and addresses us as fluid creatures will have far-reaching implications. Working at just the psychological level, too much of our organism is not attended to, and the inevitable result will be limitations in the growth we can attain.

In Continuum, we add sounds for the purpose of penetrating tissues and stimulating fluids. If you stand in front of a big gong and bang it, the sounds are intensely palpable. They vibrate tissues. The kinds of sounds made in Continuum are often vowel-like sounds such as *O* or *E*. These sounds are directed into different areas of the body. Ultimately, the sound should be sufficient to generate movement of tissue. Initially, however, the student may attempt to consciously make such movements, going slower than you can even imagine. After a while, we are listening for the movements that want to happen. It is a dance between intention and attention. In a sense, the very essence of continuum is learning to merge our consciousness with the deepest layers of our bodies. In doing so, tissues are enriched by the increasing vibrancy of their fluids.

From a Continuum perspective, the body *is* movement. We don't "do" movement; we learn to participate with, enrich, and enhance the movements that we are. Included in those movements are links to our ancestral heritage, so it is natural for those ancestral movements to arise in our consciousness. We can literally feel our primordial selves arising. We are connected to a greater life sphere; it is a universal connection. All too often, human suffering comes from having a limited sense of self. The value of these movement experiences broadens and enriches our sense of who we are.

Continuum is a secular process, yet it has a powerful spiritual dimension. It offers a tangible, realistic, and intelligent way to understand a basic premise of many spiritual traditions: namely, that we are all connected. We are connected via the water that is most of what we are and by the water that surrounds us and in which we dwell. Perhaps light and water are the most tangible manifestations of consciousness on earth.

As we engage this work, we gradually enhance our capacity for fluid resonance. Resonance carries information. It is how we can tune in to another in a very deep, whole-body way. Resonance allows two people to vibrate in each other's presence. As bodies become more fluid and more resonant, they can transmit and receive, simultaneously, a force that is delicious to experience. Again, we can call this love. It can be in a sexual context; it can also be in a loving context that isn't sexual.

Let's see it in Emilie Conrad's own words.

> *It took me many years to recognize that the undulating fluid that I felt in my body is the movement of love. Looking back, it seems so obvious—that the undulating waves of primordial motion are the movements of love. Not emotional love but an*

encompassing atmosphere of love—a love that has its own destiny.[10]

As we progress in our Continuum practice, we continue to let go of the "me" and its rigid limits and begin to sense whispers of our origin. Occasionally, there is even a sense of surrender to the divine in an almost ecstatic yielding to the sublime. The basic connection to this resonant field becomes more available. This field is the ultimate healer, the perfect mother/father. It reminds us that we are not alone. This is a felt presence, not a conceptual presence, and it is always available. It is always already here to comfort and connect. It never leaves us. Is this what the mystical teachers have called being bathed in God's love?

For a list of continuum teachers worldwide, check continuum-teachersassociation.com. If there is not a teacher in your area, or if you can't find a convenient workshop to attend, some are now teaching online. Look for one.

The third thing we are just beginning to learn about our body is the importance of the quality of its architecture: the way our structure organizes in space, how the major components relate to each other, and how well they are balanced in the field of gravity. These are factors in how we perceive ourselves in the world. Further, the nature of our life challenges, our comfort in our skin, and our personality strengths and weaknesses can be seen in the structure of the body. For example, think of a person who is slightly stooped with an appearance of slightly sunken chest. Is he someone you would guess to be confident, assertive, or forceful? Not likely. Or think of an individual whose chest is puffed out, incapable of a full, easy exhalation, and whose muscles are taut and rigid. Can you imagine him relating from a tender, vulnerable, openhearted place? Again, not likely.

Structural Integration

One day back in 1970, I read a magazine article, written by Sam Keane, titled "Sing the Body Electric." It was about the work of Dr. Ida P. Rolf. I knew immediately structural integration was for me. I had already come to believe that "body armor" had to be released for my wounds to be healed.

By 1971, my own experience made it obvious that extensive impacts and insults warp the body as well as the psyche. When I first read about the work of Dr. Rolf, I was enchanted. Ida Rolf was a triple Taurus, and no astrology buff would be surprised to learn that she could be a very direct and forceful person. From her perspective, if you wanted to change a body, well then, get your hands in there and do it! This required courage, vision, and a profound knowledge of human anatomy to manually enter tissues deeply enough to release, lengthen, and soften them from the surface all the way to the bones. Structural Integration, as she called her work, is a remarkable approach to the human body, one that has yet to be fully appreciated. Yet for those who know and have had the good fortune to experience structural integration, they know it is a gift to humankind. It is a dimension of healing that cannot be overlooked. *It addresses the coherence of the structure as a whole.* How could such changes not affect the entire human being?

To understand and appreciate the import and benefits of structural integration,[11] we need to grasp an essential concept. The body is a physical structure, and its major components, such as the head, shoulders, chest, spine, pelvis, and extremities, have a spatial relationship to each other. For example, where is the pelvis in relationship to the feet? Where is the pelvis in relationship to the shoulders? Are the shoulders level, or is one higher or behind the other? The practitioner of structural integration requires the skill to see these relationships and know which tissues have tightened to create the patterns that reduce the balance, flow, and ease in our bodies. When these relationships have been compromised, there can be profound effects on our functioning, health, and well-being. Now let's look at Structural Integration in the context of coherence.

Recall coherence is a state in which both individual autonomy and global cohesion are maximized. As an example, let's look at a shoulder. How can it be described in terms of local freedom and global cohesion? The shoulder girdle has four joints.[12] Raising our arm smoothly above our head involves not only the freedom of those four joints but also movement between the ribs and movement of the spine. For our shoulder to be coherent, we need the joints of the shoulder girdle, ribs, and spine to do what they are designed to do: move freely and in a coordinated fashion. This is true for all the joints of the body. Ideally, movement is a dance of fluid local freedom and global coordination.

Structural relationships are determined by the length of connective tissues and muscles. When the length of the tissues that flex and extend a particular joint are at their optimal length, we can say they are in balance. For example, the biceps muscles—and their fascia—flex the elbow joints; they shorten the angle between the bones of the upper and lower arms. The triceps muscles extend the elbow joints; they increase the angle, straightening out the arms. If the biceps have shortened from their optimal length relative to the triceps, the elbow joint will be chronically flexed. Both sets of tissues will be tighter than is optimal. By design, they have an optimal length and should contract fully and extend fully. Dr. Rolf says

> *Rolfing seeks to enhance function by changing structure ... We see that bones are held in place by soft tissue. If a muscle is chronically short, it will pull the attached bone out of balance. When one part is in trouble, the body as a whole gets out of balance. In a static structure, such as a house, for example, if a door doesn't swing true or close properly, it really isn't enough to rehang the door. To balance the door permanently, it would be*

> *better to look to the symmetry of the foundation. Structures must be balanced as a whole—this is as true of living structures as it is of houses and bridges.*[13]

Nature Designed the Human Body to Be Vertical

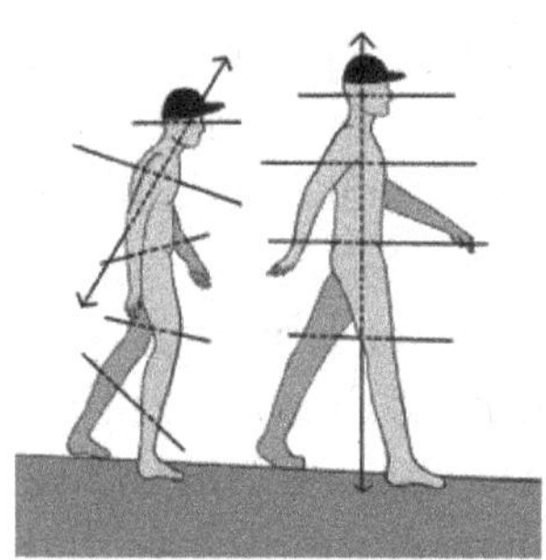

The direction of human evolution is toward the vertical. It was Dr. Rolf who first called attention to the fact that each of us lives and breathes in a field of gravity and that our physical relationship to gravity matters. To Ida Rolf's mind, gravitational energy, the field of the earth, is a source of nourishment that may reinforce and augment the field of the body. However, in order for this to happen freely and easily, the body must be in an unhindered relationship with gravity; it must be "well stacked." The body must be truly vertical, in a coherent alignment within the gravitational field.

To the degree that the human body is not well aligned within the field of gravity, we can safely conclude that the body is holding excessive amounts of tension and strain. If, for example, the head is held well forward of the shoulders, an extremely common condition, then the weight of the head is "falling" into the middle of the chest and will create tension in the ribs and chest muscles, prohibiting an easy and full inhalation and exhalation in respiration. Further, the muscles in the back of the neck must work overtime to compensate for the head falling forward. They will chronically "hold on." Remember chronic tension in the body serves as a feedback loop to the limbic system, reinforcing its hypersensitivity. This means our threshold for activation of the sympathetic system is lowered. And that is only one of the many negative effects of chronic tension; it affects our health, our mobility, our sense of who we are, and even our capacity for intimate connections. Chronic tension is, literally, a weight on our hearts.

For many years, I have observed how little children, ages three to four, sit. I have been impressed at the vertical thrust in their little bodies. Their heads reach for the sky and are aligned over their chests, which sit well balanced over their pelvises. We were born to become vertical, and it matters how well we achieve and maintain that verticality. It matters for our mobility. It matters to our psychology. And it matters to our health.

So what is it that keeps us from reaching our full length? What keeps us from occupying the fullness of our being? It is not only in the vertical dimension that we do not reach our full physical potential. It is also in the front-to-back and side-to-side dimensions. We can, literally and physically, be more filled out, and I am not referring to weight or muscle building; I am referring to a quality of fullness in our tissues and availability of inner space.

Why is it that most humans get shorter as they grow older? Why do our ribs sink subtly toward our pelvis and our heads fall slightly more forward and why does our mobility decline? For most of us, it is simply "normal" aging. Does it have to be this way? Structural Integration says no.

What we see when we look at any human body is its genetic expression in interaction with the effects of impacts, chronic insults, learned habits, nutrition, exercise, and the overall quality of the environment in which that body was reared. Obviously, genetic factors influence how we age; however, for most of us, how we age relates to how we deal with the effects of the impacts and insults that have accumulated throughout a lifetime. The more obvious impacts are physical. A breach birth, a serious fall off a highchair, an accident, and yes, even surgery can create definite and substantial effects on how the physical body coheres and how it is aligned and balanced within the field of gravity.

Let's look at a very simple impact that most people wouldn't consider worth mentioning in a narrative of their life. A young boy falls from a tree and displaces his coccyx, his tailbone. In addition, he experiences a slight twist in his sacrum. Yes, in the moment, it was an intense experience, but after a good cry and some parental comforting, this little boy goes about the business of his childhood. Now the little twist in his sacrum and the lateral displacement of his coccyx, over time, will affect his entire body. Since the muscles of his pelvic floor attach to his coccyx, they will be pulled and create a tension situation. The placement of the rest of his spine will be altered because his sacrum is its foundation. His structural integrity has been compromised, and this will create chronic tension with all its implications, including possibly an effect on the boy's sense of self. This is a simple demonstration of how a body's structure can be impacted even without the contribution of any other psychosocial life conditions.

Our structures are affected by the myriad psychological and emotional impacts and wounds we receive. When a child is told a thousand times not to express herself in a particular way, she will learn to obey that injunction by holding the muscles of that expression. For example, typical body movements accompany assertion. There is a certain freedom of movement in the arms, shoulders, chest, and face. If a child is not allowed to assert herself, she will learn to hold herself in a way that hides her expression of assertiveness. Over time, that holding will become automatic and structured into the body.

For excellent self-care, we need to understand what areas of our organism have been affected by the impacts we have received and how these effects are limiting our enjoyment of life, affecting our health and aging process, and challenging our ability to enjoy love connections. We have looked at the effects of our wounding on our psyche, our model of self, our connections, and our sense of responsibility or authorship. We looked at how these wounds affected an area of the prefrontal cortex and at how they affect our autonomic nervous system and our susceptibility to stress. Now with Dr. Rolf, we arrive at a mind-blowing understanding of the interconnectedness of the whole body and its potential for improved coherence.

Since 2007, there have been several international medical research conferences about fascia, and the data is fascinating.[14] The old image of the body was based on Newtonian physics, and it was mechanical, a conception of movement based on muscles, bones, and joints. But the picture is changing. A new image of the body is emerging. One fascinating video, which that can be found on YouTube, presented in the conference involved a tiny camera inserted under the skin. The title was *Strolling under the Skin*. And though it would be impossible to do justice in words to what was shown, I can say with certainty that any Newtonian understanding of how the movements of the body function can be gently laid to rest. The wet webbing of fascia is ubiquitous and very much involved in our movements. This film captures the fluidity and responsiveness that is happening in every direction under our skin.

The body is whole; the idea of segments is man-made. Muscles rarely transmit their full force via tendons onto the skeleton. They distribute a large portion of their force onto sheets of fascia. These sheets can extend to several joints and to several other muscles. It would not be simple to say which muscles participate in a particular movement. Rather than thinking of the more than six hundred muscles in the human body, visualize it as one muscle poured into more than six hundred pockets of fascia. Everything is connected. The more coherent the body, the more likely it is that every one of those muscles and fascia will respond to a movement anywhere in the body.

Hellerwork Structural Integration

One variant of Dr. Rolf's approach is called Hellerwork Structural Integration. For twenty years in the 1980s and 90s, Hellerwork Structural Integration was a large part of my professional practice.

Joseph Heller was president of the Rolf Institute back in the mid-1970s. A successful practitioner, he was very much in demand in Santa Monica. What made him so popular, in addition to having highly skilled hands, was he always dialogued with his clients while working on their bodies. His work was about people, not only their bodies. Therefore, when he decided to leave the Rolf Institute in 1978 to open his own school, his emphasis was to teach his practitioners to address the whole person. The bodywork itself was exactly as he had learned from Dr. Rolf; however, by focusing on the person, a different quality of experience emerged, reinforcing the correct idea that body and person are not separate.

Practitioners of Hellerwork are concerned with how the body expresses its psychology. In Joseph's words:

> *As Reich, Lowen, Feldenkrais, and others have recognized, people are always perfectly self-expressive through their bodies, both consciously and unconsciously, advertising their attitudes and beliefs in their postures and movements.*[15]

Hellerwork Structural Integration is done in eleven sessions, and a different theme was developed for each session to help the client understand how her body reflects her life and to provide a starting point for dialogue within the session. For example, in the first session of the series, much of the work focuses on the area of the chest and diaphragm. A typical result is greater ease of breathing. Thus, the theme given to this session is "inspiration."

The direction of the dialogue is not preset; it might be about relationships, self-esteem, confidence, and so forth. However, by beginning with the theme of inspiration, the client not only gets a physical experience of more ease in breathing, but also an understanding that the breath is related to feeling inspired in life.

Themes for the other sessions include "standing on your own two feet" for the session in which the legs and feet are addressed. As the sides, arms, and shoulder girdle are being released, the theme of "reaching out" may begin the dialogue. We have looked at the importance of the fight/flight mechanism. The arms and legs are vital to the activities of fight/flight. The feet and legs ground us in relation to the earth, and the arms ground us in relation to people and things. This is the kind of information clients learn during the Hellerwork series. In each session of the series, as different aspects of the body are attended to, a new understanding or experience can be brought into conscious awareness.

Since the whole person is the focus in Hellerwork, it also became the guiding principle in how Hellerwork Structural Integration was taught. It was not just the passing on of skills; the student was central. Hellerwork training is about helping each student learn more about herself, learn how to be present, and learn more about how to be in relationship to her clients.

What is it that makes Hellerwork education a unique skill learning experience? It is the "space" that the teacher creates through her *being* and *skills.* The space refers to the vibrational field that is created in any relationship. In the Hellerwork classroom, the trainer creates it by

- recognizing the importance of maintaining a safe atmosphere for learning
- remaining centered, open, and attentive
- maintaining an energetic link to each individual and to the group as a whole
- carrying both a personal and impersonal energy; this refers to an attitude that is both quite personal and friendly and quite impersonal and in charge
- giving nonjudgmental feedback
- knowing how to encourage student's self-disclosure and participation
- seeking to nurture student's strengths
- moving fluidly from academic presentation to personal process and back again
- not fearing the unknown and being willing to engage with whatever arises and use it for the class's benefit

- carrying the quality of authority without being authoritarian
- having firm but flexible limits, expressed in words and actions

I want to insert a caveat as I conclude this discussion of the work of Dr. Ida P. Rolf. Many people have told me that they did a ten-session series of SI bodywork. Most say it was good, and that was that. Why has it not become an ongoing part of their health regimen? In the early days of the work, when the only school was the Rolf Institute, practitioners told their clients to get ten sessions, or maybe fourteen if they wanted to include an advanced series of four sessions. Before I was trained, I asked Dr. Rolf why her practitioners did this. I added that I had already had over forty sessions and that my body was continuing to improve. She responded, "Of course, your body is going to continue to get better, but there are 250 million people in this country and only two hundred Rolfers." I took a deep breath and thanked her for her honesty.

As of today, I personally have had over four hundred structural integration sessions and have no plans to discontinue. Now at seventy-nine, I deeply appreciate how this work has contributed to my posture, the fluidity of my movement, and my health and well-being.

We've come a long way since the 1930s when Wilhelm Reich was preaching the necessity of addressing the body in psychotherapy. Yet after all these years, we are just beginning to understand the importance of addressing our body in our adventure toward wholeness. Over centuries, there have been many factors retarding our ability to live in a body that is fluid, structurally integrated, and capable of feeling delicious through the mere acts of walking, dancing, and even sitting. For most of us, this may sound like fantasy. Those factors have included the necessity to tame a harsh environment (the process of evolving civilization); the lack of comprehension about our body itself, including the technology to "stroll under the skin"; the phenomenal assortment of insults and impacts that most of us are subjected to throughout a lifetime (traumas, abuse, war, neglect, and the consequences of the lack of emotional intelligence); and finally, the unavailability of disciplines and practices to change the situation. All that has changed.

We no longer need to tame our environment; we need to learn to live in harmony and balance with it. The comprehension, technology, disciplines, and practices are becoming more and more available. The single most important factor is to want to and intend to realize our fluid integrated potential.

Resources

The Novato Institute for Somatic Education
Also, Google "Feldenkrais," "Functional Integration," or "Awareness through Movement."
The Hellerwork Institute
The Guild for Structural Integration
ISMETA

Notes

1. See *The Body of Life* (1980), *The End of Tyranny: An Essay on the Possibility of America* (1976), and *Bodies in Revolt: A Primer in Somatic Thinking* (1970) to appreciate the depth and importance of Hanna's philosophical writings.
2. Hanna, T., *Somatics: Reawakening the Mind's Control of Movement, Flexibility and Health,* Perseus Books, 1988.
3. For more information about Susan Harper, who is among the finest teachers I have ever met, see www.continuummontage.com.
4. Ho, Mae-Wan, *Living Rainbow H2O,* World Scientific Press, pp. 4–5.
5. Conrad, Emilie, *Life on Land: The Story of Continuum,* North Atlantic Press, pp. 290-291.
6. Pangman, M. J. and Evans, Melanie, *Dancing with Water: The New Science of Water*, pp. 2–3.
7. Conrad, Emilie, *Life on Land: The Story of Continuum,* North Atlantic Press, pp. 290-291.

8. See Pollack, Gerald, *The Fourth Phase of Water,* Ebner and Sons, 2013, for a complete discussion of this phenomenon.
9. Ibid., p. 119.
10. Conrad, Emilie, *Life on Land: The Story of Continuum,* North Atlantic Press, pp. 320-321.
11. There are several schools of structural integration, including the Guild for structural integration, Rolfing Structural Integration, Hellerwork Structural Integration, and Kinesis Myofascial Integration. Although different in flavor, all are branches off the tree of Dr. Rolf's insights and techniques.
12. The shoulder girdle itself, consisting of the shoulder blade and collarbone; the scapulothoracic joint for the shoulder blade's movement in relation to the upper ribs; the sternoclavicular joint, where the collarbone (clavicle) meets the breastbone (sternum); the glenohumeral joint (the true shoulder joint), where the upper arm comes into the girdle; the acromioclavicular joint, where the clavicle meets an extension of the shoulder blade (the acromion).
13. Rolf, Ida, *Rolfing and Physical Reality,* Healing Arts Press, 1978.
14. Findley, Thomas, "Fascia Research from a Clinician/Scientist's Perspective," *International Journal of Therapeutic Massage and Bodywork,* Vol. 4, No. 4, 2011.
15. Joseph Heller, *Bodywise,* Jeremy P. Tarcher, Inc., 1986, p. 83.

12

The Emotional/Psychological Dimension of Wholeness

Everything flowers from within of self-blessing.
Though sometimes it is necessary to
reteach a thing of its loveliness,
To put a hand on the brow of the flower
and retell it in words and in touch,
"You are lovely"
Until it flowers again from within, of self-blessing.
—Galaway Kinnell

Human beings create abstractions that nature doesn't abide. The deeper we look, the more obvious it becomes that our body, our psychology, our relationships, and our spirituality cannot be separated. Even the expression "whole organism" is insufficient, because there is no such thing as an organism outside relationship. Relationship is not merely relationship to other humans or mammals in general, but also to the natural world and to one's sense of what can be called a Superior Power.

In this chapter, we will consider a range of approaches to

healing the emotional/psychological dimension of self. When I walked into a psychiatrist's office in 1964, I believed psychotherapy would fix me. A few years later, I realized that "fixing" was a whole-organism project. This change in perspective began with my introduction to the work of Wilhelm Reich. Sadly, his work is not well-known or studied today. I believe this stems from the adamant desire to keep the body and the so-called "mind" separate and compartmentalized.

Reich was a medical doctor and a sexologist when he became a student of Freud. In my years of undergraduate and graduate psychology, not one of my professors mentioned his name. Yet his influence has been vast and far-reaching. His thinking went far afield from the psychology of his day—a true visionary.

One of Reich's major contributions[1] to the psychoanalytic field was his work in describing what he called "character structures," or patterns of protective mechanisms composed of consistent attitudes and behaviors that served to protect the person from painful feelings. This understanding of character or personality patterns was a huge breakthrough in the field, and Reich's status soared. The idea that an individual's character (i.e., the *how* of his mannerisms) could have a protective function was easily palatable to Reich's contemporaries. These were emotional, attitudinal, and behavioral patterns well within the domain of psychoanalysis—the talking therapy. However, the more Reich ventured toward including the body, the more ostracized he became professionally. And then, with his next step, he ushered in the demise of his reputation.

Reich claimed that the character of the individual was functionally identical to the structure of his body. This means that observing an individual's body would enable the therapist to know the nature of his character and the patterns of his resistance. Chronic tension patterns and chronic personality mannerisms have the same function. They are protective and block the free flow of energy. Chronic muscle tension binds sexual energy, it binds anxiety, and it binds anger. Further, to resolve the conflicts from which the individual suffers, the tension patterns in the body must be released. These tension patterns were mechanisms of coping with the conflicts that were at the root of the disturbance. For example, the association of sexual pleasure with moral guilt could result in both chronic bodily tension patterns and character patterns that bind and inhibit the free flow of sexual or life energy. Reich was pointing toward and describing the *organism as a whole*. The conflicts and inhibitions are not simply psychic. *They are structured into the body as well!* This came to be called *body armor*.

I have taken workshops with descendants of Wilhelm Reich. I have watched these therapists stand individuals up in front of a group and, looking at their mostly unclothed bodies, describe their childhoods and their major issues and challenges. As a beginner in the area of the body, I was amazed when the individuals corroborated the therapists' readings. Reich believed that if an individual could not experience a full, whole-body release in orgasm, the undischarged energy would organize itself as symptoms or disturbances. This ability Reich believed to be the hallmark of good health. He believed that an individual should be able to build a very strong charge throughout the whole body during the sexual arousal process and then, in orgasm, release the entire charge. Healthy orgasm should be an almost cosmic experience, in which the individual loses the sense of himself as a separate being. From Reich's point of view, when a person achieved this, he was "healthy."

The therapy Reich developed involved four components.

- Deep breathing. Different kinds of breathing exercises are used in this therapy. A primary purpose is to build a charge of energy in the body. As the charge builds, the therapist notes where the individual is constricting his body and not allowing the charge to move through.
- Expressive movement exercises. Pounding a bed with your fists or kicking it with your legs while verbally expressing something like "No! No!" There are a couple of objectives here. One is to move the energy where it is not moving well.

The other is to incorporate into the individual an expression that has been stifled in his personality.

- Massage areas of the body that contract as the client intensifies breathing. The obvious objective is to free up these areas.
- Psychological analysis. Reich was a psychoanalyst and believed in the method. Today, there are still some traditional Reichian therapists in the world, but they are far and few between. The offshoots of Reich are far more common, and their methods of doing psychological work vary a great deal.

Three of the primary descendants of Reich whose work is available in many countries are Alexander Lowen, John Pierrakos, and Eva Pierrakos. Dr. Lowen was a student of Reich's. He founded a system he called Bioenergetics. Lowen included exercises that were designed to move energy and to build and release "charge" from the body.

Dr. Pierrakos was a long-term associate of Lowen. Eventually, as is often the case with gifted collaborators, he began his own system, which he called Core Energetics. Whereas Lowen was concerned with the physical, mental, and emotional levels of the patient, Pierrakos added a spiritual dimension. His vision of the human being was broader than was his mentor's. Pierrakos's wife, Eva, also began her own system, which she called Pathworks. A Google search can locate practitioners of Bioenergetics, Core Energetics, and Pathworks in numerous countries. Wilhelm Reich directly influenced all three.

Healing Overwhelming Impacts: Dr. Peter Levine's Somatic Experiencing

Throughout this book, I have referred to the whole organism or the whole human being, including relationship skills and capacities, belief structures, identities (or one's sense of self), physical structure, and movement. Each of the visionaries I have chronicled contributed to our understanding an aspect of the whole. Dr. Peter Levine is another who has made an enormous contribution to our comprehension of what happens to the body—particularly the autonomic nervous system—when an individual is overwhelmed by fear and helplessness or by shock trauma.

Reich was a psychoanalyst, not a somatic practitioner; nevertheless, his contribution was seminal. Healing must consider the body as well as the psyche! In classroom talks, I heard Dr. Levine say he has attempted to stand on the shoulders of Wilhelm Reich. Both Reich and Levine understood that the autonomic nervous system was compromised when there was significant stasis in the structure. Reich attempted to release the body and defensive patterns while restoring autonomic equilibrium via high intensity breathing and explosive expressions or catharsis. Levine did just the opposite. He realized that the best way to restore the autonomic nervous system's functioning with highly traumatized human beings is to work with very small amounts of excitation and very small releases. These discharges were homeopathic in size compared to Reich's.

To understand Levine's contribution to treating the living body as a whole, let's examine a hypothetical situation. Rob is an extraordinarily healthy being, having had an excellent upbringing that included much love and care. Impacts and insults were minimal. Then, one day he suffered a massive trauma. He was mugged, beaten, and tossed in front of an oncoming vehicle. When the ambulance arrived, the EMTs were highly functional; they treated him efficiently but like an object as they had no comprehension of the psychophysiological effects of trauma. Through the skill of the medical staff and the wizardry of modern medical technology, Rob lived. However, the intensity of this impact *could* have ushered in a full-blown, posttraumatic stress disorder (PTSD), even though previously Rob had been robust in every sense of the word.

If an individual like Rob is not given the proper trauma care and allowed time to "discharge" the shock, he could have symptoms and difficulties for the rest of his life. As Dr. Levine explains,

> *The nervous system compensates for being in a state of self-perpetuating arousal by setting off a chain of adaptations that eventually bind and organize the energy into "symptoms," such as: hyperarousal, constriction, dissociation (including denial), feelings of helplessness, hypervigilance, hyperactivity, exaggerated emotional and startle responses, nightmares, mood swings, reduced ability to deal with stress, difficulty sleeping.*[2]

A variety of symptoms can emerge over time, but this example gives you an idea of some of the long-term effects of serious trauma. This single high-impact incident, uncomplicated by an early history of serious impacts and insults, is the kind that is best treated by the Levine system.[3] Throughout his study, Dr. Levine looked to animals in the wild for inspiration. He observed that these animals often were subject to near-death experiences. Strangely, however, if they escaped death, they did not suffer PTSD. Why? And why do humans who endure similar fates so often develop PTSD symptoms? To understand the answers to these questions, we must return to the *polyvagal model* of the ANS and review what occurs when there is a high-impact traumatic reaction.

In chapter 8, we saw how social engagement is the first line of defense against stress. The ability to "feel and deal," to self-assert, to ask for support, and to share one's vulnerabilities are all stress protective. This means that at the level of the nervous system, it is the ventral vagal complex that mediates these activities. If the mechanisms mediated by the ventral vagal system are compromised, our next line of defense is the sympathetic nervous system with its fight/flight mechanisms. This is how we protect ourselves.[4]

In the kind of high-impact events that Dr. Levine describes, the sympathetic nervous system and the fight/flight mechanism are overwhelmed. The organism cannot marshal the resources to fight or to run away. First, there is a sudden halt of movement, an arrest, characterized by extreme vigilance and scanning to orient for the danger. Next is an attempt to escape. If this is not possible, there is an attempt to fight. But if neither flight nor fight is possible, all that remains is to freeze, to become scared stiff and/or collapse. Let's use Peter's words to describe exactly what he calls a trauma. "Trauma occurs when we are intensely frightened and are either physically restrained or perceive that we are trapped. We freeze in paralysis and/or collapse in overwhelming helplessness."[5]

This freeze response is mediated by the dorsal vagal complex and involves the viscera to a great degree and the heart to some degree. In preparing to fight or flee and not being able to, all the muscular tissues tighten and remain tight. In addition, with freeze, the guts and organs also tighten. There are several reasons for this defense. In the wild, there is a chance that the predator will conclude the prey is already dead and not want to eat "dead meat." Or the predator might get careless and allow the prey an opportunity to escape. At the very least, the prey won't feel the pain of becoming lunch. Nature, in its mercy, has designed a mechanism so the prey can dissociate, "not be there," for his final fate. This is an act of dissociation in which our consciousness leaves our tissues.

How many millions of individuals have suffered an impact of this degree? Many types of events can result in such a traumatic reaction. Rapes, muggings and beatings, automobile accidents, falls, birth traumas, war traumas, and even surgery can cause this reaction. How many millions of individuals walk around never having resolved the impacts they may have knowingly or unknowingly received? They walk around in a state of contraction with both their sympathetic and parasympathetic systems stuck in high gear.

However extreme the example of dissociation given above may be, many human beings walk the earth in a partial state of numbness, unaware that their essential nature is fluid, sensual, and erotic.[6] Our essential nature is life flowing. However, just one impact of extreme intensity, or thousands of much lesser intensity, will strip us of our birthright to be the vibrant, strong, awake, loving, sensual, erotic beings that nature intended. We are designed to be self-regulating and to *digest* experience. With a regulated, resilient system comes the experience of "I can," of being able to handle life. There is a sense of having options, of feeling connected to ourselves, and being able to enjoy life and deeply relax. High-impact trauma and/or an accumulation of life's wounds interfere with the best of what life offers.

In addition to bringing forth a psychobiological understanding of what happens when an individual is subject to a high-impact traumatic event, Peter Levine has also developed a method for its treatment.[7] Instead of plowing into the middle of the traumatic experience or talking it through, somatic experiencing first establishes "resources" and links them to sensations in the body. The trauma itself is titrated a little bit at a time to gradually discharge the vast pent-up energy, restore the biological defenses, and restore self-regulation and equilibrium.

Psychotherapy

It wasn't many decades ago that only so-called "crazy people" went to a psychotherapist; there had to be "something wrong with you" to consider such an intrepid act. Even today, when millions upon millions of individuals and couples regularly visit a therapist's office, a faint hint of suspicion still exists. From my perspective, finding and working with a good therapist is an act of great intelligence. You don't need to be depressed or suffering from intense anxiety or have an addiction to receive a great deal of benefit from a course of psychotherapy. Of course, if you are experiencing those things, even more important to find a good therapist. In any event, it can be an enriching experience and help you enjoy close relationships even more. Self-knowledge is the nature of this journey, this road toward wholeness, and psychotherapy can be a great resource.

All human beings need good relationships to thrive. But here is the Gordian knot: good relationship skills are learned. To have good relationships as an adult, it helps a great deal if your parents were able to be present with you, empathize with you, and attune to your emotional needs. Think back to how children have been treated for centuries, and it is easy to understand why human beings everywhere are challenged by relationships.

For me, the decision to look in the Yellow Pages for a psychotherapist saved my life. I was twenty years old, in the air force, and drinking myself silly. After awakening in the back seat of my car at 5:00 a.m., bleeding from my throat due to outrageously excessive drinking and hollering, I knew I needed help. The type of therapy I received in those early years is best described as psychodynamically oriented, which meant the therapist listened to me talk about my problems and attempted to provide meaning within a framework first established by Freud.

On one hand, very little change occurred in that work; however, one single comment by my therapist, Dr. Lou, made all the difference in my world. The dialogue went like this: "I want to major in psychology, but what would I do with a bachelor's in psych?""Get your PhD." "But I barely went to high school." "You can do it."

Wow! If this Harvard-trained MD psychiatrist thought I could do it, what if I could? A window of possibility opened.

This conversation took place in 1964. In 1967, I began a doctoral program in clinical psychology at the University of Kansas. Dr. Lou was right. I could do it. He was able to see me and hold a higher view of me than I could. This is one of many gifts a therapist can offer. From 1964 to 2012, I experienced and studied a variety of different approaches to psychotherapy. All contributed to who I am today, both personally and professionally.

Diana Fosha and Accelerated Experiential Dynamic Psychotherapy

Of all the psychotherapies I have experienced and studied, the most humanly relational one I encountered is called Accelerated Experiential Dynamic Psychotherapy (AEDP).[8] Dr. Diana Fosha is the founder of this approach. It is elegant, effective, and very relational. What makes this approach so beautiful is that it explicitly and without shyness states that therapy is about growth and transformation, not merely about treating symptoms. It is about helping people live more fully, engage in life, work, and love. AEDP isn't content with symptom alleviation and stress reduction; it aims higher—toward thriving, flourishing, and resilient functioning.

AEDP explicitly aims to provide those ingredients that so many human beings did not receive in their first primary relationships. As an infant and young child, we require a good dose of an adult's presence, someone who can be there emotionally and who can welcome us into the world and delight in our being. We need someone who can attune to our feeling states and meet us there; we need someone who can support our deeply ingrained motivation to grow. We need someone who has the capacity to be present with us, empathize, feel what we feel, and support our emotional explorations and development. To the degree that these basic needs are not met, we suffer.

From the very first moment, AEDP therapy seeks to provide what was missing. Almost all schools of psychotherapy emphasize, to some extent, the importance of the therapist offering unconditional positive regard, empathy, and warmth. This is more front and center for some approaches; others keep it more in the background.

In all my years in the field, I have never encountered a psychotherapy that so actively extends warmth, support, acknowledgment, and affirmation as AEDP. The typical client enters therapy accustomed to living within the confines of the protective structures he created in childhood to minimize the pain of not having his essential needs met (or worse). These protective structures are now a source of pain. Love, resonance, and the good vibrations of others have a hard time penetrating and touching their heart. Based on many years of experience, I have come to believe that a lack of love reaching the heart is a root cause of so much human suffering. This is a lonely way to live.

The AEDP therapist generously and profusely offers loving words and feelings. She may meet the client with empathic prizing such as "I'm just so amazed at the courage you showed in standing up to your father. That couldn't have been easy." Each time the therapist makes a comment like this, she carefully observes the reaction of her patient. Usually, she will notice that the client deflects, blocks, or minimizes the care that was just extended. We humans rarely recognize the difficulty we have in receiving love. Instead, we ascribe our deficits to others not extending it. Letting love in is an almost universal challenge. Gently and with care, the therapist helps her client become aware how he is deflecting the good stuff. Thus, a profusion of validations and affirmations—sincerely offered—not only provides a climate of real safety, making it much easier for the patient to soften his protective structures, but also makes it clear just how the patient goes about keeping at bay the very thing he most craves.

A beautiful moment during such therapy is when the client lets the therapist touch his heart. It is a special moment for both therapist and client. Something new has occurred. The client feels seen and valued; he begins to recognize he is genuinely loveable. I have witnessed anxiety disappear from a client's daily life as the recognition of his worth grows session by session. As his protective structures melt, he discovers his worth and lovability, but more than that, his deep inner strength and a sense of mastery begin to grow.

Dr. Diana Fosha coined a term, *transformance,*[9] to refer to the motivational drive toward wholeness, coherence, contribution, and connection. From the very first session of therapy, the therapist looks for the manifestations of transformance, however subtle they may be. For example, a client might describe his awful feelings, and the therapist acknowledges his courage in sharing them with another human being. Throughout the AEDP process, the therapist strives to recognize every moment in which the client's fundamental drive to wholeness shows up.

This approach is different from those that focus on the problem, seeking better ways to think and act or seeking to work through all the negativity and arrive at what's positive. Fosha's approach is to build the positive first. Eventually, those highly distressing and incomplete feeling experiences will surface and be addressed from a positive base; in AEDP language, "self at best" deals with "self at worst."

When individuals who have not experienced a successful intimate love relationship come in for therapy, the work is to help them feel safe enough to let their protective mechanisms down and disclose their vulnerabilities and their tenderness, as well as access their strengths and assertiveness. The work helps them learn to receive and accept authentic praise, affirmations, and acknowledgments from others—to let love in.

Sometimes it is difficult to take in and absorb what we most long for. As a little boy, I recall kicking my grandmother if she tried to hug me. I craved affection, but I was simply incapable of allowing it. The pain associated with not receiving what I needed, and especially the pain associated with receiving the awful stuff I didn't need, made it hard to accept love when it was offered.

Many years later, in my personal AEDP therapy, I found it enormously helpful to have the depths of my experience felt and seen by another and to have my strength validated. I was able to receive it. The experience of being deeply seen is a fundamental need. Many of us live with that longing. Yet fulfilling it often requires not only someone willing to see but also willing to help process the pain closely related to being seen.

A beautiful feature of AEDP is the therapist's willingness to verbalize her own feeling experience. Many approaches shy away from this out of fear of blurring boundaries. Yet what the client most needs, what he has never had, is a real, genuine relationship experience in which he is prized and cared for. For example, the therapist might express her fondness for the patient or the pain she feels in seeing how difficult something is for him. Whatever the expression, she then explores how the client was affected by it. Recall how important it is for an infant to have the moment-to-moment engagement with its mother, communicating through facial expressions via the heart and the right brain. The absence of such attunement insults the organism. When the AEDP therapist offers it openheartedly and plentifully, it invariably evokes conflicting responses. When it does and the client is able to consciously see them, the opening has begun.

Some of the most poignant moments I have experienced while doing AEDP are when I simply say something like "I am so sorry that happened to you." When such an expression is honest and sincere, the client can feel that someone really is there and experiencing their feelings with them. The therapist might help the client verbalize these relational moments. The following is an example: Therapist: "What do you see when you look at me right now?" Client: "Kindness." Therapist: "How does it feel to see me looking at you with kindness on my face?"

In traditional psychotherapy, the therapist is usually more passive. She doesn't judge and is kind and understanding, so over time, the client will likely feel close to his therapist. In AEDP, however, the therapist actively and immediately works to establish an intimate relationship with the client. The therapist establishes a good, intimate relationship with the client—someone who doesn't yet have the skills to establish a good, intimate relationship. In the process, the therapist names and amplifies the client's every small success. A new, secure, and successful relationship is being established. In this context, the old emotional wounds are brought forth and worked through.

There is another ongoing goal in the work of AEPD. When shame, guilt, and fear block our access to our deeper feelings and resources, we invariably feel very alone. Our inability to access and process these inhibitors is what keeps us stuck. Thus, a central objective of AEDP is to undo the painful sense of aloneness that our clients live with. In many ways, the message expressed is "I am here with you. Can you feel me here with you?" The client's growing sense of not being alone is part of the healing process. By having another who can witness, hear, understand, attune to, and empathize, the client can work through the things that hurt them and develop a sense of resilience and mastery in the process.

In AEDP, the client learns to participate in a shared experience, gets validation for his responses, and sees someone who is present with him and communicating nonverbally with a focus on feeling. For example, the therapist might reflect, "Your tone just changed, and I had an uneasy feeling you were moving away." The client is strongly encouraged to articulate what he notices about the therapist's nonverbal communication and how it makes him feel. I can still feel my AEDP therapist's presence as a force of solace and support.

In AEDP, the therapist pays exquisite attention to the client's somatic responses. Changes in skin color, facial expression, sighs, shifts in breathing, changes in head position and posture, and tone of voice are some of the signs illuminating the therapist's way. This requires the therapist to remain exquisitely attuned to the moment-to-moment changes in the client. It is not too dissimilar from a mother gazing into her infant's eyes and responding to the minute changes of feeling and expression revealed.

A simple exchange I had with a client will serve as an example. After I expressed how moved I was by what she had just revealed, she sighed. "I noticed a deep sigh," I said. "I wonder what you were experiencing." She responded, "It felt like I had just released something I have been carrying for a long time."

Another of Dr. Fosha's brilliant therapeutic innovations is to alternate between processing and metaprocessing. In essence, metaprocessing is a reflection upon the experience just completed. We want clients to take home their experiences and to integrate them and reflecting on them with the therapist helps them do that. Their mutual reflection then may become a takeoff point for another round of experiencing. The following is an example: Therapist: "How was it for you to see the delight on my face when you asserted so powerfully?" Patient: "It was great. I've never had anyone pleased when I came across like that." If the therapist notices some expression that suggests that for a small part of the client it wasn't so great, she asks about that, ushering in another round of experience.

From my perspective, AEDP is the most caring, relational, and outright loving therapy out there. At the same time, it is deeply rooted in neuroscience, relational psychology, and psychodynamic theory. The first time I heard Dr. Fosha speak, I thought I had never met anyone who embodies both sides of her brain in such a thorough and fluid way. I knew I needed to experience and study her work. Professionally, AEDP has influenced me more than any other system. My work has become more effective and much more enjoyable.

AEDP trainings are being held for therapists in different parts of the United States and the world. I urge you to check out this approach. Your life will be richer for it.

Hal and Sidra Stone: The Psychology of Selves and Voice Dialogue[10]

I think I said this before, but somebody up there likes me. When a boy grows up bullied by his mother—intimidated, threatened, beaten, and humiliated—he more than ever needs a father to be there for him. When the father is passive, withdrawn, hostile, or humiliating, a great gap is left in a young boy's psyche. Pain and inadequacy live where confidence and competence should. It is not a very good way to go through life. Filling this gap wasn't easy, but over and over again, I had the good fortune to encounter strong and loving men. From each, I took something that filled the void.

Hal Stone was one of those men. Rugged and ruddy, he looked

more like a Greek sea captain than a Jungian analyst. At the center of his teaching was the importance of owning and supporting our vulnerability. It may have been harder to hear that message had it come from someone who looked less masculine than Hal.

Hal and his wife, Sidra, began developing what they call the Psychology of Selves and the Voice Dialogue method in the mid-1970s. Their aim wasn't to develop another school of psychotherapy but a system of awakening consciousness—an extraordinary contribution to the process of becoming whole. We humans are much more than we take ourselves to be. We tend to limit ourselves by identifying rather rigidly with a constellation of beliefs and attitudes that constitute our sense of who we are and who we are not. The story of the lion who took himself to be a goat is the perfect metaphor to illustrate this. Too many of us are lions but walk around believing we are goats.

Let's look at Hal and Sidra's concept of "selves" or "parts." We have seen that we are fluid creatures with the capability of shifting in a variety of ways to meet novel conditions or necessities. For example, in the boardroom, we can be decisive, unequivocal, and analytical. In the bedroom, we can be sexual, playful, and sensual; we can be dominant, loving, hot, submissive, tender, sweet, or caring. Day to day, we might be practical, rational, and empirical, or we might be intuitive and mystical. We can be vulnerable, playful, innocent, or any combination. These are all "a different feeling sense" of our body. Obviously, some attributes will be dominant while others much more recessive. Ideally, we have access to our less dominant qualities, but all too often, they may be hidden.

An individual might identify with the rational, serious, and practical part of him and leave little room for a part of him that is intuitive, playful, and romantic. These "selves" are then "disowned." It is as if we are saying they are "not me." However, there is more to this story. The people most likely to upset us are those who carry our disowned qualities. Let's say assertiveness is a quality we have disowned; then we tend to be more accommodating, perhaps even passive. But guess what. Individuals who are clearly assertive are likely to annoy us.

It isn't as if we should have every opposite quality in equal measure. Ideally, we can have access to qualities that are not our dominate one. The decisive, rational individual could access and engage his playful, intuitive, or childlike side when the situation calls for those qualities.

To skillfully facilitate the emergence of these undeveloped aspects of self, the facilitator needs not only skill and compassion but also the ability to access these parts in herself. The "vulnerable child," for example, is an aspect of self that is precious and contributes enormously to our ability to experience genuine intimacy in our lives. Yet the wounds of childhood often leave this part buried under a mound of protectiveness. That protectiveness can take the form of a controlling personality or an overintellectualized or critical "self." In fact, the individual who is fiercely critical of self and others is usually one whose vulnerable self was deeply wounded. In this situation, the facilitator would first establish rapport with the critical self and reflect her understanding that this self has good intentions, namely, to protect the individual from pain. Then she would gently invite the vulnerable self into dialogue with the intention of opening space for this precious aspect to emerge.

The work of the Voice Dialogue method is to bring into consciousness those parts of us that have been disowned or insufficiently developed. At the same time, it strives to reduce the influence of those parts that have been overdeveloped, such as the "pusher," the "pleaser," the "perfectionist," or the "critic." Parts that tend to be disowned or underdeveloped are the "vulnerable child," the "power self," the "laid-back self," or the "lover."

Becoming aware that different aspects have different "energetic" qualities is a beautiful feature of the voice dialogue process. This links directly to the "feeling sense" of the body. For example, the facilitator may ask to speak to a part of the individual who has been submerged by the inner critic. Let's say the lover. This part will have a very different feeling tone, a different vibratory quality, from the inner critic. This is what Hal and Sidra Stone refer to as *energetics,* and it involves attunement to the felt-sense of the part.

To get a full sense of human possibility, Hal and Sidra turned to Greek and Roman mythology to describe aspects of self. For example, Aphrodite, the goddess of love, might be a part the facilitator asks to speak to after speaking to inner critic. Again, this is not just a mental conversation. The facilitator uses her own Aphrodite quality to evoke the same feeling tone in the client. If this part in the individual has not developed, he essentially gives birth to this new dimension of self with the facilitator as midwife.

The Voice Dialogue method awakens the ability to "hold the tension of opposites"; Hal and Sidra Stone consider embracing "and" consciousness, a hallmark of maturity. If an evangelical minister could only acknowledge how good it would feel to sleep with someone he met at a party *and* that it is against his moral values, he could hold that tension without letting it snap and getting caught at the local brothel.

We can become aware of and embrace selves we have previously disowned. When we do, we won't have to find other people to hold our projections. The hatred directed toward certain groups is an example of abhorring an aspect of self. Instead of owning the loathed quality as an aspect of self, we project it onto another and hate it in them. Obvious examples are the sexually promiscuous or the entire LGBTQ community. Whether we agree with their values is not the issue. If there is hatred or disgust, it indicates a projection. As Hal and Sidra Stone put it, it is time to embrace ourselves. As we do, we become more coherent and better capable of loving self and others. Here's an example. I had always seen myself as a "nice guy," perhaps ironic when my boyhood dream was to become a professional prize fighter. Nevertheless, aggressiveness was "not me," and I intensely disliked aggressive people. Perhaps it's obvious how this would limit my sense of self and be a source of conflict with others. It wasn't until I was able to accept my own internal "killer" that I could open new space within and grow my own sense of strength. Reclaiming a disowned aspect is an empowering experience.

Back in the early 1990s, while directing a Hellerwork Structural Integration Training, we introduced the Psychology of Selves system. After introducing the system academically, we did the following ritual. Sequentially, each student spent time in the "hot seat" while the class, led by the teachers, identified how the student presented himself in the world. What was his or her primary identity (or subpersonality, to use Hal and Sidra's language)? One student, a man named Harry, had been a construction worker prior to becoming a student in the Hellerwork training. On first appraisal, he could be a bit intimidating. He had a thick, black beard and very dark hair. His shoulders were broad, and despite a full series of structural bodywork, they were not exactly what I would call fluid. He usually wore blue jeans, flannel shirts, and jean jackets, giving the overall impression of a man's man. He looked tough, rugged, outdoorsy, rigid, remote, emotionally unavailable, and supermasculine. These were some of the adjectives the class used to describe him.

Next in the process, the class was to pick a set of qualities that represented an opposite of those Harry presented in his day-to-day life. After some deliberation and experimentation, the class agreed the perfect opposite was a flamboyant, gay interior decorator we named Armando. To our surprise, Harry agreed to play the role. Everyone in the class was given their opposite character to play. They were given the afternoon off to go to town, find costumes, and come to dinner as their new characters. We would have dinner in character and a dance afterward, also in character. There was no contesting the winner of the best male actor that evening. Harry, as Armando, had shaved his beard, cut his hair, and found colorful and expressive clothing. He entered the dining hall wearing a bright-pink sarong, jewelry and carried a very strong feminine affect. He never once came out of character the entire evening. We were impressed and awed. What was even more stunning and equally edifying was that, when he danced as Armando, *Harry's shoulder girdle moved with a fluidity and grace we had never seen in him.* Harry's image of himself, who he took himself to be, did not include moving with ease and grace. Yet when he adopted Armando, he could!

The next day, he came to class as himself, and it was interesting to note that his shoulder girdle appeared as it usually did, only perhaps a little bit softer. However, the change in Harry's life over the ensuing years has been nothing short of amazing. He is a congruently gentler man, and he gives ample attention to the artistic side of himself. *Identity can limit movement, feeling, and being.*

Bruce Ecker and Coherence Therapy[11]

Coherence therapy attempts to remove symptoms with laser like efficiency. Its central concept that of the "Pro-Symptom Position," is an important one for therapists to be familiar with. Essentially, it warns against attempting to remove a symptom without first knowing how that symptom is serving the patient. For example, a patient presents with the symptom of anxiety. Using one of several techniques, the therapist discovers what occurs if the anxiety were to simply disappear. Often, the client realizes how the anxiety is serving to protect him from facing his vulnerability. The therapist would then help the client find effective ways to face the vulnerability and thus no longer need the anxiety.

Albert Terry Sheldon, Beatriz Win-Stanley, and CIMBS (Complex Integration of Multiple Brain Systems)[12]

This is another highly relational approach to psychotherapy that has profoundly influenced the way I work. In many ways, it is similar to AEDP, except the patient is invited to maintain eye contact with the therapist throughout the session to the best of his ability. The patient is invited to remain in present time, attending to his experience and sensing what it is he is feeling and wanting. Obviously, this can be challenging for some patients.

We have seen how the ideal relationship is experienced as maximum individuality (differentiation, freedom) *and* maximum closeness (the jazz band metaphor). This is a very evolved state of integration. Asking a patient to be as fully with his "self" as possible—*and* in connection with the therapist—is asking him to move toward coherence. In this process, all that interferes with or compromises the patient's coherence gets revealed.

Psychotherapy is an educational, healing, relational, and consciousness process with the potential of benefitting us greatly. I consider it an essential component in this journey of a lifetime.

Notes

1. For a thorough consideration of the work of Wilhelm Reich, see *Wilhelm Reich: Selected Writings* and *The Function of the Orgasm* by W. Reich.
2. Levine, Peter, *Waking the Tiger,* North Atlantic Books, p. 145.
3. In the more typical situation of an individual with a moderate to severe history of impacts and insults who shows up after a high-impact event, Levine's method is best used in the context of a relational psychotherapy, in my opinion.
4. I refer the reader back to chapter 11 for a review of the polyvagal model of the autonomic nervous system.
5. Levine, Peter, *In an Unspoken Voice,* North Atlantic Books, 2010, p. 48.
6. When I use the word *erotic*, I do not mean it in the way the word is commonly used. I am speaking of a highly relational, pleasurable connection to life itself.
7. See Levine, Peter, *In an Unspoken Voice,* for a beautifully detailed explanation of the process.
8. Fosha, Diana, *The Transforming Power of Affect,* Basic Books, 2000.
9. Fosha, Diana, *AEDP: Transformance in Action*, Excerpted and modified from Fosha (in press). In K. J. Schneider (ed.),

"Existential-Integrative Psychotherapy: Guideposts to the Core of Practice," Routledge.

10. See Hal and Sidra Stone's *Embracing Our Selves; Embracing Our Inner Critic; Embracing Each Other;* and *Partnering* for a thorough exposition of their work.
11. See Bruce Ecker *Depth-Oriented Brief Therapy* (now called Coherence Therapy) and Ecker Ticic and Hulley's *Unlocking the Emotional Brain* for a full presentation of Ecker's work.
12. Sheldon, Beatriz and Sheldon, Albert, *Complex Integration of Multiple Brain Systems in Therapy*, W.W. Norton, 2022.

13

The Relational Dimension of Wholeness

A delicious intimate relationship can be among the finest rewards of embarking upon and remaining in the commitment to our own evolution. So many teachers and books tell us the work we must do is within us. "Personal growth," "Embodiment," or "Spiritual evolution" is "my" work. Yet so much of where our challenges lie as human beings can only be seen in the context of relationship.

I am thinking of a patient who worked with me for a couple of years. She was a "model" patient. In each session, she did a piece of personal work that seemed to further her growth. She began a new relationship, which quickly became rocky. She then requested some couple's therapy. Within two sessions, it became obvious that all her good individual work had barely touched the skills she needed to have a successful intimate relationship. A new level of work had begun.

The committed, sexual relationship is the best venue to discover what's hidden in the basement of our consciousness. It grants the best opportunity to learn what we need to develop, what we need to recognize about ourselves, what we need to let go of, and what we may need to forgive.

Over the years, I have known many people who by virtue of their personal work arrived at a place where they felt good about their manifestations in the world. In so many ways they were thriving—with one big exception. Their lack of a satisfying intimate, sexual relationship was leaving them feeling less than whole. Some of the most common types of challenges I've witnessed include not being able to find or sustain a relationship; being in a relationship for years but it is always on the verge of ending because sexual or emotional intimacy is missing; one partner or the other doesn't feel seen or understood; the couple functions well together but each is either lonely or bored or there's been a betrayal that can't seem to be healed. Often, these relationships hobble along because the fear of the pain of ending, and the fear of being alone, are greater than the dread of continuing in this unhappy state.

One of the richest aspects of this healing adventure is the potential to evolve an ever-deepening relationship replete with openhearted intimacy and an ever-exhilarating sexual relationship. It takes commitment and self-awareness at every level of our being—somatic, psychological, relational, and spiritual. It takes courage, willingness, resilience, self-regulation, and a modicum of skill.

We enter life in relationship. America is the land of rugged individualism, where "my freedom" sits on the peak of our value system. Yet there is really no such thing as "me" without "we." For the first several years of our lives, we literally cannot survive without caretakers. We are social beings. Social isolation is among the most severe forms of punishment. We need each other.

From the moment of conception through birth and the first few years of our lives, our relationships are the context in which we form our concepts of self, of others, and of the world. These models will be the guideposts for our future intimate relationships. Are people trustworthy, or should we be very cautious in revealing ourselves? Do our needs generally get met, or does it feel hopeless when we have an emotional need that requires another? Can we really be close to someone and still have our autonomy, or are we afraid we'll be smothered or even abandoned? Is our strength, sexuality, and intelligence safe to show others? Clearly, our deeply held concepts hugely influence the course of our relationships.

For the most part, these beliefs are unconscious, and unless we commit to their discovery, they will tend to remain so. As anyone dissatisfied with their intimate relationship will tell you, it's definitely their partner's fault. "If only she [or he] were different." How many times have I heard this refrain? It's when we begin looking in the mirror, with sincerity and compassion that we begin to uncover our own contribution to our relationship difficulties.

It is clear and obvious that the quality of the relationship between infant and parents is critical to the infant's psychological development. Yet in the 1960s, that assertion made world-famous psychoanalyst John Bowlby a heretic in his profession. Until Bowlby, the general assumption was that the infant is a package of biological drives that can be tamed and channeled in the process of development; parents mediate and intervene between the cultural prescriptions and the infant's instincts. Further, disturbances arise when internal conflicting drives within the infant are not well negotiated. In other words, in those days the emphasis was intrapsychic, meaning that the conflicts or challenges were within the psyche of the child and had little to do with the actual relationship between child and parent. Later known as the father of attachment theory,[1] Bowlby turned the world of psychoanalysis around with his emphasis on the relationship itself as a primary driving force within which the personality developed.

His work was seminal, generating volumes of research over the years. In recent years, it has provided a theoretical framework for many systems of psychotherapy, both individual and marital therapy. It is a helpful framework within which to understand adult intimate connections; it also provides a way to make sense of distressed relationships. Bonds are classified as secure or insecure. When a marriage is characterized by lots of distress, almost always one and often both partners have had an insecure bond with one or both of their parents.

The fundamental questions—the answers to which determine whether a relationship is secure or insecure—are the following:

- Can I count on you if I need you?
- Will you be there for me emotionally?
- Is it safe to be me?
- Can I express what I feel?
- Will you meet my needs in a timely manner?

If deep in her heart a child can answer yes to these questions, if there is sufficient acceptance, presence, and emotional connection, the child will feel safe in the relationship. She will feel secure and have no need to be vigilant and guarded. Her parents provide a secure base from which she can explore her world and a safe place she can return to repeatedly for comfort and nurturance.

There are profound psychophysiological differences in children who are quite securely bonded with both parents versus children who are insecurely bonded with one or both parents. Our capacity for sustaining satisfactory intimate relationships as adults is momentously influenced during these early years of bonding.

Optimally, a secure base and a safe haven are constructed in the relationship between caregiver and baby. It is from this secure base that the toddler begins to venture forth to explore his world. The mother of a securely attached child is available when the child returns from an adventure and can appropriately respond to provide modulation and regulation. It is to this safe haven that he returns for nurturance, comfort, and reassurance. For many years, life will be a series of excursions and returns. When the quality of the bonding is secure, that security is internalized as a very fundamental core sense of "I am OK. The world is a safe place." The "I" is rooted in this core sense, and it allows for risk-taking in exploration. It allows for a willingness to be open and reveal oneself. The secure toddler knows that distress will be comforted and hurts will be soothed.

A good foundation is present! In adult intimate relationships, those who were provided a secure base and safe haven will have the internal structures to provide that for their partners. Also, they will have a much better chance of not contracting a chronic illness. When you have a secure base and a safe haven in your partner, you will feel free to live your life to the fullest, knowing that when you are bruised in the world there is a place of solace. It is in this context that the child develops a good internal regulation system. Initially our parents serve the function for us as we do not yet have the neurological or psychological structures to take it on.

This internal thermostat is the sine qua non of satisfying adult relationships. People whose internal regulator doesn't function well will have difficulty controlling impulses, be moody, and might not handle frustrations and demands well. Further, a good thermostat is necessary to allow real closeness or to permit distance. Closeness can generate intense feelings at times. A good internal regulator allows you to modulate those feelings so that they don't either drag you to the bottom or have you bouncing off the walls.

As adults, those who were securely attached as children have a much better chance in intimate relationships. There are two dimensions in a relationship that each couple negotiates—mostly implicitly—on an ongoing basis. These are closeness and power. Adults who have experienced a secure relationship as children can manage these negotiations with greater ease and less distress. They can enjoy closeness, and they can enjoy solitude. They can accept differences, argue, and work out issues without reacting as if the world is about to end. They can be in charge or be the one who knows or the one who decides in some areas; alternatively, in other areas, they can feel comfortable following their partner's lead or having their partner know more or make decisions. There is fluidity in the power and closeness dimensions, a give and take. Each can feel free internally and simultaneously closely connected to his partner. In other words, the relationship leans toward coherence.

Ruptures occur frequently even in very good relationships. A rupture is when the filament of closeness, that sweet thread of heart connection, is frayed, diminished, or fractured. Ruptures can be huge or very tiny, such as the irritation we might feel when watching our partner load the dishwasher the exact opposite way we do. In good, secure relationships, the ruptures are quickly repaired. It is important that we are able to identify ruptures and become skillful at repair. This requires paying attention to the quality of the ongoing connection between you so that you can know when repair is necessary.

Insecure Attachment

In contrast to securely connected children, insecurely connected kids live in a different kind of psychosocial world. Three types of insecure attachments have been identified.

In the *avoidant* insecure bond, it is as if the young child has concluded that his needs are not going to be met, so why bother? Expecting to be rejected, he shuts down or withdraws from the relationship. Mothers of avoidant infants are likely to subtly block and reject the infants' bids for comfort. Therefore, to protect themselves from the pain of not have their needs for comfort or emotional contact met, these children are likely to express minimal feeling and to be withdrawn or hesitant in their interactions. They tend to avoid physical contact.

As adults in intimate relationships, they are the ones without apparent needs. They act as if they don't need anything from their partners except to be given freedom from the other's emotional demands. They have learned to push away experiences and feelings they don't like. They can appear independent or autonomous, but in attachment terms, they are compulsively self-reliant, meaning they are afraid to be dependent on anyone. Underneath, they often feel inadequate; they are afraid they don't really measure up and find it hard to believe that they can be truly loved. Deeper still, they long for acceptance.

In another style of insecurity, the child seems preoccupied with Mom's presence and shows little interest in exploration and play. This style is called insecure preoccupied or insecure resistant. As adults, these children may desperately cling to relationships, thinking their security lies out there somewhere. "Are you there for me? Are you going to leave me? My world revolves around you. What can I do to make you happy?" They can appear loving, close, and intimate, but in attachment terms, they lack healthy individuation or healthy boundaries and may be compulsive caregivers. They can also be highly critical, especially of their partner's lack of emotional engagement. They are inclined to undervalue themselves, not knowing their own self-worth, their own natural goodness, or what they genuinely have to offer others. Of course, underneath, they are lonely and quite sure that no one will really be there for them. Deeper, they are longing for someone to really be there for them.

As ways of being in relationships, both the avoidant and the insecure-preoccupied styles can vary in intensity, ranging from slight tendencies to deep entrenchment. In my years of counseling couples, one of the most common patterns I have seen is one in which one partner—frequently the woman—displays what we have called the insecure-preoccupied pattern. She will be the one who insists on counseling, is frequently angry at her partner, and complains about his emotional unavailability and lack of commitment to the relationship. Her husband, exhibiting the avoidant insecure pattern, will lament that if only she weren't so emotional, so easy to upset, then everything would be just fine. He will present as having his emotional life together, stable, and calm. However, as counseling proceeds, it doesn't take long to uncover that he is afraid and feels inadequate. His façade covers those feelings with an "I don't need anything" attitude, yet underneath, he is scared. Even deeper, he longs for her acceptance and approval. She, on the other hand, is covering deep loneliness with her rants as well as fear that no one will really be there for her—that she will not be able to depend on him. She feels unlovable and longs for her mate to show up and provide that reassurance, presence, and love. If he begins to come forward, however, she will be pushed up against her fear of being unlovable.

When the couple can come to recognize their deeper feelings and needs and communicate them to each other, they can create a secure bond. As long as they continue the conversation at the level of their self-protection—their complaints against each other—they will simply reinforce their sense of insecurity in the relationship. From the perspective of coherence, as they become more authentic, they can begin to feel both cohesive as a couple and free as individuals.

There is one more style, and it is the most severe. Generally, it is associated with abuse or serious neglect. What happens when the very one who, biologically, is supposed to be a haven of protection, comfort, and nurturance is instead a source of danger and threat? The internal conflict becomes intolerable!

This individual is likely to have a great deal of freeze[2] in his system. As an adult in relationships, we may see vacillation between clinging, avoiding, and aggressive outbursts. Often there is a communication message that reads, "Please come close to me. I dare you." One patient I recall would simply disappear, get in his car, and leave the state for weeks or even months whenever the emotional heat in his marriage became intolerable. However it manifests, the pattern is usually extreme. Clearly, I entered adulthood entrenched in this pattern. Any signs that my wife desired closeness would result in my picking a fight over the most inane and trivial subjects. Closeness was intolerable, but so was distance. The marriage spiraled to divorce. Decades passed, a couple more marriages quickly came and went, but I had begun the journey and there was much healing work to be done. Now at seventy-eight and in the thirty-seventh year of a marriage that gets richer in every way, I write about what it takes to have such a marriage.

We've seen how identity, connection, and responsibility are

three dimensions of being that all of us can continue to grow. Let's see how our wounds in these three areas show up in relationships. Rigid identities are a good place to begin. If, for example, I have to always be tough, in charge, a man's man, then I exclude experiences of receptivity, yielding, and receiving pleasure. It might be hard for this person to be empathic or a good listener. I am not saying it's bad or wrong to be a no-nonsense, in-charge individual. I am saying being wed to this persona without the capacity to shift to others is extremely limiting and can be highly problematic in a relationship.

Another common example of a rigid identity is a person who always has to be nice, pleasing, or accommodating. Again, this can be a wonderful persona if this person can also disagree, assert, or express a contrary opinion, when the necessity arises. It's the rigidity of identity that usually is the problem, not the fact that this person is usually a certain way. (Obviously a criminal, psychopathic identity in and of itself is highly problematic.)

It is commonly recognized that we all tend to pick partners who in some significant ways are opposite to us. For example, a not uncommon configuration goes like this: He is rational, organized, punctual, and sequential. She is intuitive, artistic, and flows with time. Initially the differences are attractive, but when the honeymoon glow wears off, the differences begin to drive each other crazy. Until, that is, they realize they are each other's teacher. If each can embrace some of the other's qualities, each will have a fuller and richer sense of self. Moreover, they will no longer drive each other crazy as they come to appreciate the differences. Each can expand to include and become enriched and more whole. The culture's lack of comprehension regarding polarities and the human ability to embrace "both/and" is a wounding in and of itself.

Our body is essentially water. We have known this for a long time. What we haven't known or considered are the implications of this simple biological fact. *Our essential nature is fluid!* As we have seen to the degree that our bodies are sufficiently open, sufficiently fluid, and sufficiently coherent, then life itself is a source of nourishment. We will have more ability to shift out of any particular identity and have more options and a wider variety of ways of being. One can be funny and playful when appropriate, tough and decisive when appropriate, sweet and accommodating when appropriate, and so forth. Our relationships become much richer than if each person is locked into a given persona with little breathing room.

I've been fascinated by the recent emergence of the nonbinary phenomenon. I wonder if we are witnessing the awkward beginning stations of a tectonic shift in identity constructs. I'm not suggesting nonbinary is the way of the future. I believe male and female are biological givens, but the constructs that tell us how to be male and female may be undergoing profound changes. Think of water, vapor, and ice. Imagine them as metaphors for the capacity of both male and female to radically "shape shift." This is what the future may bring.

Let's look at this through the lens of coherence. What would a coherent and fluid identity look like? Each of the many parts of our personality would have the freedom to be a voice at the table, and each of our parts would be cohesive with the whole. Taking this to the level of relationship, each partner would feel fully autonomous, and each partner would feel amazingly close to the other. Perfection here isn't the goal, and coherence is not a static state. There is movement back and forth. Sometimes partners need more space, sometimes more closeness, and sometimes alone time.

Our feeling sense or connections to our body is one of the elements determining the quality of our connection to others. We maintain rigid or incoherent identities by disconnecting from parts of our body and by chronic tension. We can grow this capacity regardless of our age, but we have to understand its importance first. The absence of an immediate, moment-to-moment, feeling-sense connection to our body is a limiting factor in our self-awareness. The unknown areas of tension and disconnection support the locking in of identities. Here's an example on the rather extreme side. Let's say a person's attitude toward sexuality is "I never even think about sex unless my husband and I are ready to have another child. Then I do my duty." How is that sense of self even sustainable given what sexual creatures we are? Simple! All it takes is to cut off the connection to our pelvis; no aliveness there, no sensations, no problem.

It is a similar process with the individual who is always "in charge, tough, and manly." Just make the rib cage rigid and unyielding enough and the job is done. *Our ability to experience and the quality of our tissues are related.* Once the tissues harden, the choices become limited. If I can't let go of my rib cage, it's hard to let go into soft, yielding feelings. Let's look at one more cultural wound—the lack of understanding that we are the author our own story. "Who should we blame?" How often do we hear this question? In our personal lives, the tendency to blame the other—rather than examine our own contribution to the situation—is nearly universal. Even when we blame ourselves, there is usually the implication that it is because of what the other has done to us. Ignorance or insufficient understanding of our essential nature or identity, our connectedness, and our authorship are just some of the elements of our "cultural wounding."

Then there are thousands of years of stifling, sensuality-killing patriarchy. We have subjugated women, and of course, as they have begun to emerge and claim their full humanness, the road to male-female harmony has much to be worked out. We have subjugated the earth. Popes over the centuries have sanctified invasions and empire building in the name of converting the heathens. Our own country was founded by the descendants of conquerors who destroyed indigenous civilizations. No wonder the rugged individualism of the Wild West still thrives in our body politic. All this is the soil of our individual births and formative years. So even in our most loving homes (not to mention the possibility of coming into the world with issues from past lives), we all have work to do to come close to achieving the potential of our intimate relationships.

The Work That Must Be Done: Comprehension, Integration, Maturation, and Practices

There is no one way to have a satisfying relationship. I've known couples who fought frequently and were very happy in their marriage. However, they didn't hold grudges and there was no contempt expressed in their fights. I've known couples who never fought, always agreed, and were miserable. I've known couples who rarely "shared their feelings" yet deeply enjoyed their relationships. That said, I do believe that our intimate relationships can be a source of emotional satisfaction, sexual pleasure and exploration, identity expansion, and perhaps most of all, self-discovery. Further, none of this needs to be curtailed by age. As someone once said, we don't stop playing because we get old; we get old because we stop playing. So whether your relationship is satisfying, distressed, fun, lonely, or nonexistent, healing the wounds of childhood and culture can certainly include evolving our relationships toward deeper emotional intimacy, creative and adventurous monogamy, self-discovery, friendship, and purpose. The following are practices, and they are ways of being in a relationship. Often a good course of couple's therapy is required to really begin to embody these. Often, they require changing how we understand things.

Speaking from the heart.

I remember being asked to "speak from [my] heart" when I was a student in the Hellerwork Structural Integration Training. I had no idea what was being requested. I could hear a difference when others were able to, but I had no idea how to get there. One day, sometime later, I did! I was talking to a friend. It was a feeling. I could feel the difference. I could feel how there was a clear connection with the other person. Initially, I had no idea how it came about.

Speaking from the heart is a lifelong work. It carries a vibration of truth and requires us to soften what psychoanalysts call our defense mechanisms—intellectualizing, rationalizing, projecting, blaming, repressing, and overidentification with particular aspects of self. This last one may need some elaborating. If I am overidentified with the nice girl or boy, which means it is outside my self-concept to be forcefully assertive, my ability to speak from my heart is limited. It's limited because speaking from the heart requires me at times to be forcefully assertive. Said another way to the degree that my sense of self disallows any particular dimension of being—for example, forceful, playful, sensual, vulnerable, rational, intuitive, erotic, tender—this ability to "speak your truth" is compromised. In other words, to speak from the heart requires engaging the journey of healing.

I want to emphasize one aspect of speaking from the heart that makes all the difference in a sustained intimate relationship: vulnerability. Here's an example. John and Carol are at a party. Drinks flow. John's dancing for the third time with Mary and getting physically closer with each dance. Carol is seething, finds Joe, and begins dancing provocatively with him. On their drive home, the fireworks and mutual recriminations begin. This is an example most people can understand and relate to. What might it look like if both John and Carol could speak from their hearts and own their vulnerability? Let's say Carol begins. "I was so pissed watching you with Mary. I felt jealous and scared and then wanted to punish you, so I got even by dancing with Joe. It's really important to me that you consider my feelings. I want you to be aware of how you are affecting me in those situations. What was going on with you?"

John might respond, "You're right. I was moving in really close to Mary. I did want to hurt you. For the last week, you haven't welcomed me home once with a hug. I was feeling distant from you, lonely, and wanted to punish you. Next time I will do my best to let you know when I'm missing you."

Owning our vulnerability means to recognize and acknowledge those tender feelings of loneliness, missing the other, fear, jealousy, and envy. It simply means acknowledging what's true. Many of those feelings don't square with our sense of self, so we pretend they don't exist within us. We lie! To tell the truth means expanding our sense of our self—our identity—to make room for what was previously forbidden. It takes strength to own our vulnerability. We open ourselves to looking weak, being shamed ("If you were a real man, it wouldn't bother you"), feeling raw, or stepping into the unknown with a sense of no control. Nevertheless, the ability to engage at this level is what allows a marriage to be a great one. Here's another example of how owning our vulnerability requires strength. "When I tell you I'm afraid and you roll your eyes, it makes my blood boil. I need you to be respectful when I express vulnerable stuff to you." All said with a strong, no-nonsense tone of voice.

Recall the model maximum individuality and maximum togetherness or closeness. Learning to stay with ourselves, to know our experience, our truth, *and* connect from there to another is the path to awesome relationships. Learning to recognize what we are feeling and what we are needing, then to communicate from our feelings and needs rather than with automatic reactions, is to live in a whole new world. Again, even in families where everyone feels secure in their relationships, where do we learn to do this? We cannot "be ourselves" without embracing this key aspect of ourselves. Human beings are vulnerable; we are the only species who knows our time here is finite and that those we love will also pass on.

Repairing ruptures.

Understanding and becoming skillful with the process of repairing ruptures is important in all significant relationships. It is important for spouses and for friends, and it is important for parents and children. When there is a rupture in the connection or a break in that warm, positive sense of the other, it is time to reestablish it. Here is an example. Mother and infant are gazing lovingly into each other's eyes when the infant unexpectedly tugs on Mom's hair, causing a sharp pain. With highly evolved video equipment, we can see the split-second look of anguish and fury flash across Mom's face and fear on the baby's face. It doesn't last more than a fraction of a second, but it is visible on the monitor, and both feel the momentary disconnect. When a smile quickly returns to Mom's face and baby registers it by smiling back, the rupture has been repaired. What is important here is not to allow those moments of hurt or anger to fester and accumulate.

We cannot live with another person without occasional disagreements, disappointments, and especially minor annoyances. This sounds simple, and in one sense it is. However, for people whose prefrontal cortex and autonomic nervous systems were compromised, little annoyances quickly escalate or are hard to let go of. So we must make it a conscious priority and remind ourselves, again and again, that what is important is strengthening our connection to our loved one, not being right or justified in our annoyance. This can take muscular effort, but it can be done, and the rewards are immeasurable.

Release frustrations, irritations, and disappointments quickly and gracefully.

This is very much related to the ability to repair. A client of mine has been struggling with his reaction to people who don't wear a mask during this COVID pandemic. Whenever he sees someone maskless, he wants to punch them in the face. Clearly, a visceral response is completely understandable. However, early in treatment he was unable to let go of the internal agitation for hours. This is poor regulation, and in his case, his wife would vacillate between getting mad at him and withdrawing from him. Magnify this to several times a week, and it's clear how his inability to let go corroded his marriage.

What's required here? Intention, commitment, and support.

We have to want to learn to not let things eat away at us for inordinate lengths of time. Instead of telling ourselves we're justified and it's the fault of "those ignoramuses," we must bring the force of intention to bear on our challenge. Each time we fail, we must have the commitment to return to our intention with firmness but also compassion. Shame-inducing self-criticism only exacerbates the difficulty of overcoming this destructive habit. Further, we need support. As a client recently said to me, "No one likes going into the dark basement alone." Understanding that we were not given the nutrients to grow the structures of self-regulation, and that it is not too late, can facilitate self-compassion. The holding of a "supportive other" is frequently necessary to develop this essential relational capacity. This is sometimes referred to as dyadic regulation or soothing ourselves with another. For many of us, turning to another for comfort when we are upset can be extremely difficult. It places us in a vulnerable position. Yet those who take the risk learn just how helpful it can be.

Learn to self-soothe.

Dyadic soothing, self-soothing, and the ability to let go of negative experiences are important aspects of self-regulation—an absolutely critical capacity for highly successful relationships. Talk to yourself gently and clearly. Guard against self-talk that induces self-pity, feelings of victimization, or defensive anger. Listen to how you speak to yourself. In what tone does your inner voice speak? Is it harsh, demanding, or critical? Is it self-indulgent or excusing? How would you speak to yourself if you really liked yourself? Sometimes, it is important to be firm and clear. Sometimes, it's important to be comforting. Sometimes, it's important not to speak at all, just to feel and be. The ease with which we can self-soothe is related to how we were soothed as tiny children. Were our parents able to lovingly comfort us when we were distressed? If it's hard for us, then we acknowledge it's hard and commit to changing it.

No need to spend valuable time bemoaning what we didn't receive when that time is better spent giving ourselves what we didn't get. Hard? Yes, but eminently doable. Paying attention, committing, being firm, gentle, and patient all contribute.

Listen, attune, and be empathic!

One of the simplest and far-reaching gifts we can give to another is to listen. So often when we are in conversation, we can hear what the other is saying; however, we are often busy formulating our response to what they are saying. In that case, our listening is superficial. Human beings are starved to be heard, seen, and understood. So many walk around in emotional pain, feeling as if we've never been really seen or understood. Couples who are distressed, perhaps contemplating divorce, almost always feel as if they are not understood, that no one is really listening.

Step one is to focus on the other, not what's running through our mind. Just listen. The next level of listening is attuning, a highly refined listening in which it isn't just the content that is heard but the vibrational frequency with which the content is expressed. Think of a mom at a moment when she is really in sync with her baby. There is a mirroring done automatically. You can feel the togetherness and the baby's response to Mom's presence. It's resonance; it is life-giving. Most of us have had less than the desirable amount of such attunement. We might still be craving it viscerally without any idea of what it is we desire. It's powerful stuff.

How do we give it? How do we learn to attune to our loved ones? The answer involves learning to listen with our whole body. Learning to be really present, with our hearts, guts, face (not controlling the expressions that want to emerge), our whole body. It requires a willingness to be affected by the other and to feel close to the other. For many of us, both are big challenges. Yet these are also the rewards of this journey. Most of us have probably been in conversations where we felt really "gotten." Even if the other person hardly spoke, we may have felt as if she understood every word. It is a very satisfying feeling. It is receiving the gift of someone's presence.

Empathy can both result from and be independent of this deep listening. It simply means letting your friend know you get what they are experiencing. "That must have really hurt when ..." "Yeah, I get it ..." So often in our intimate relationships, one of us will express some difficult feelings or painful situations and just want empathy. Too often, our partner—rather than offer a simple, empathic response—will offer solutions and attempts to "fix" the situation. This is more typical of males, but I've seen it both ways. It's frustrating to be on the receiving end, not getting what we want and getting what we don't.

For some people, being empathic comes naturally. It sure didn't for me as I had never received any growing up. When your friend is sharing an experience with you, ask yourself, "How must that have felt to her? How must she be feeling now about that?" Then check it out. Your attempt to "get" her experience will usually be welcomed, and even if you are not exactly spot-on, your friend will clarify her experience to you. Your connection strengthens. Listening, attuning, and empathizing are relationship resources that go a long way to building an awesome relationship.

Choose your response; don't just react.

This may be the most challenging of all our practices. It is also the most powerful in terms of promoting self-development. The story of Dr. Victor Frankl is among the most inspiring stories of courage and wisdom that I have ever come across. Victor Frankl was a Jewish psychiatrist and author in Austria during the reign of Hitler, when he and his family were captured and placed in a concentration camp. His entire family was killed, and his papers and books were burned. What else can be done to a human being?

As horrendous and painful as these experiences undoubtedly were, they did not crush Frankl's spirit. We might say that he became enlightened as a result. Here is a quote from his marvelous book *Man's Search for Meaning:* "Between stimulus and response there is a space. In that space is our power to choose our response. In our response lies our growth and our freedom." Practice choosing your response. If our mate, child, or employee disappoints us and we are just at the edge of launching a verbal barrage of berating and belittling, we can pause. Count to ten. Speak from our heart after we have calmed down. Ask ourselves how we want to be in our relationships. Do we want to be the one who blows up, criticizes, and puts down? Or do we want to be able to speak clearly and firmly, with care and consideration? Believe me: it is so much easier for me to write this sage counsel than it is to practice. It's the violin of musical instruments. It's so beautiful when done well, but getting there requires great patience with those squeaky efforts.

Remain centered while engaged in difficult conversations.

Let's ask ourselves, "How well can we do this?" Subjects concerning sexual likes and dislikes, attractions to other people, money, family, and vacation plans can all be anxiety-provoking subjects of conversation. If we make a habit of avoiding these talks, distance may develop gradually over time. Secrets may accumulate and the clear space between us, where love can readily flow, fills with smudges and smears. The relationship begins to lose its vitality. We may still be comfortable and functional with each other. We may even have regular sex, but we pay a price, an expensive price, for our avoidance. We must be willing to be uncomfortable and/or to allow our partner to be uncomfortable. If I can stay centered and remain open, available, and receptive, my partner will likely be able to stay engaged in the conversation as well, even if initially very uncomfortable. How then can we stay centered?

Developing the somatic dimension of our being is one of the secrets of being able to remain centered in difficult conversations. If we can keep part of our attention in our lower body—our abdomen, pelvis, and legs—it will help keep us centered. If we can feel the support of our lower body, feel the strength of our back, we can more easily guard against flying off into reactivity. And it can also help us guard against collapsing or melting down or ratcheting up if our partner flies off into reactivity. This is our fear, that one or both of us will fly outside ourselves into deep distress. It's what motivates us to avoid all topics that can potentially result in an emotional disaster. It's a very understandable motivation, yet a costly one. It's a great feeling when we do it for the first time.

Another key is to consciously intend for the conversation to result in a closer connection. We may sweat, our partner may get upset, but the intention we set is to have this challenging conversation lead to a more profound understanding of each other and a closer feeling. Finally, know that each practice in this chapter and throughout this book supports all the other practices. Success in one will bleed into the others until we begin to realize we have improved in all of them.

Cultivate an attitude of affection, gratitude, and appreciation.

The more emotional dollars we have in our relationship account, the easier it becomes to navigate the difficult moments. We can learn to be generous in our expressions of affection, appreciation, and gratitude. We can learn our partner's love language and give abundantly. We can challenge our partner to receive and know that we all have our limits in our ability to receive. Nevertheless, we should also give to the edge of your partner's ability to absorb. Include your partner's body. So many of us have learned to be stingy in expressing our admiration, pleasure, and enjoyment of looking at, feeling, and tasting our partner's body. Go for it! Make room for some wildness!

If we want to live in an environment that feels good, that contains humor, care, delight, and affection, it is up to us to create that environment. Lots of people respond to this suggestion with "It takes two to tango." I suggest a more useful attitude is "It takes one to tango." If we can keep the focus on what is positive, if we can be generous in expressing appreciation and gratitude, if we can feel free to acknowledge what our partner means to us, our chances for reciprocity along the same lines are so much higher.

Make room for new aspects of ourselves to emerge.

As we have clearly seen, who we are carries a tapestry of possibilities. If we are unaware of aspects of ourselves, especially those we deem to be unacceptable, they tend to erupt unexpectedly. Alternatively, we may constrict ourselves in an effort to cut that part of ourselves away. If we can recognize those parts and embrace them, our sense of ourselves expands and conflicts can resolve more organically. In our essence, we have the capacity of moving fluidly among different "selves" as called for by the situation. There are two good ways to approach this practice. One is to see our partner as our teacher. Likely, she or he carries qualities we have disowned. Here is a simple and clear example. My wife and I walk into a new store. Her first thought is *What can I buy for … [whomever]?* Whether it's a grandchild or daughter, the focus is on someone other than herself. I walk into that same store and my first thought is *What can I buy for myself?* In effect, she has historically overemphasized "other," while I have leaned too heavily into "self." Our choice is to get annoyed with each other's tendency because we don't embrace it ourselves; or we can see each other as teachers. Over the years I have become much more conscious of "other," and she has become much more conscious of self.

The second way to approach this is with judicious use of the word *and.* For example, I can be tender when called for *and* assertive when called for. I can be silly and playful when appropriate *and* quite serious when necessary. If we find we can't move out of a particular way of being—for example, if we are always serious, regardless of the circumstances—then this is an area for us to develop. Another way of understanding this is being unable to move into another aspect of self is a type of imprisonment. It is a loss of freedom and literally of the ability to move. If, for example, I cannot assert myself forcefully, all those movements associated with the action of assertion are cut off from my cache of possibilities.

If, as I have been contending, we are on this planet to engage the journey toward wholeness, then this is among our most important tasks: opening to the possibility that there is a lot more to us than our initial sense of self as an adult. There is a lot more in our relationship capacities, our psychological being, our somatic being, and our spiritual being. This entire book is designed to help us travel further on the road to wholeness, knowing that our destination never ends.

Engage in mindful self-care.

It is our responsibility to take care of ourselves, to listen to our heart, to care for our body, and to honor our nutritional and spiritual needs. It is our responsibility to handle what needs to be handled. If we were cared for well as children, it is generally easier to care for ourselves as adults. As a very young adult, my ideal breakfast was a piece of chocolate cream pie along with a piece of banana cream pie and three cups of coffee with sugar. I also figured getting up from the couch to change the channel on the TV constituted sufficient physical activity. Yes, self-care did not come easy, and for many of us, it is a huge undertaking. What could be more important?

These ten practices of developing capacities are so much of what life is all about. It would be quite a group of skills if we could:

1. learn to speak from the heart and embrace our vulnerability
2. repair ruptures
3. quickly release irritations, frustrations, and disappointments
4. learn to self-soothe
5. learn to listen, attune, hear the music between the words, and be empathic
6. to choose our response and not mindlessly react
7. remain centered in difficult conversations
8. learn to cultivate affection, gratitude, and appreciation
9. welcome new aspects of ourselves to emerge as life conditions change
10. engage in mindful self-care

As more of us develop these abilities and wisdom, we will live in a different world. This is what is needed, and it should be more than obvious at this juncture of our lives in this world.

It would be sheer hubris of me to claim mastery of them; however, I can assert without any hesitation or doubt that in my late twenties I would have been classified as retarded in most areas, if such a classification existed. Today, however, that is clearly not true. It is possible to change and grow substantially! It is truly life's greatest adventure.

There is one more "practice" I want to discuss. So many couples I have seen over the years have stopped making love or do so very infrequently. They claim they're too busy, too tired, and have a host of other reasons. I suggest they schedule a two-hour block of time every week, preferably not a time they're likely to be exhausted. The objectives of the two hours are connection and pleasure. The guidelines include no specific agenda; the range of expression can be from simple kissing and touching to intercourse, making eye contact, conversing, not criticizing, and holding this time as sacred. If something comes up and a scheduled time doesn't work, then reschedule it for the same week. Make it a top priority.

Notes

For couples seeking marital therapy, I highly recommend couple's therapists who are certified in the work of Dr. Susan Johnson. It's called Emotionally Focused Couple's Therapy, and it is brilliant in shifting the focus from who is at fault to identifying the pattern or dance cocreated by the couple. Personally, for couple's therapy, I wouldn't go anywhere else.

1. For in-depth treatment of Bowlby's attachment theory, research, and application, see the following texts: Ainsworth, M., Blehar, M. C., Waters, E., and Wall, S. (1978), *Patterns of Attachment: A Psychological Study of the Strange Situation*, Hillsdale, NJ: Erlbaum Books. Cassiday, J., and Shaver, P. (ed.). *The Handbook of Attachment: Theory, Research, and Clinical Application*, Guilford Press, 2010. Johnson, Susan, *Emotionally Focused Couple's Therapy*, New York: Guilford Press, (2002). Fonagy, Peter, *Attachment Theory and Psychoanalysis,* Other Press, LLC, 2001.
2. Recall "freeze" is a response to trauma in which fight or flight is overwhelmed and the organism's final option is to freeze.

14

The Spiritual Dimension of Wholeness

To describe the journey toward wholeness as life's greatest adventure without including spiritual development would be like describing the joys of skiing without mentioning snow. Without the recognition that we are each related to and influenced by the divine, a universal force, or universal intelligence, our adventure will be limited. Our consciousness of self will be local—*my* body, *my* psyche, *my* relationships. Yet even the most secular among us sense or just wonder about how we are connected to nature, to the sun, moon, and stars, and to each other. Of course, we can live a very good life without spirituality, especially if we have done our psychological, somatic, and relational work; nevertheless, there will be vistas unseen and sublime feelings unfelt.

Huston Smith, the eminent scholar of world religions, compared living exclusively in the cosmology of Newtonian scientific materialism to living in a cave, versus living in the great outdoors.[1] We can build a beautiful and spacious cave, but it is not the outdoors. A spiritual understanding is the most beautiful context in which to do our somatic, psychological, and relational work.

In the first edition of my book, I spoke little about spirituality. I've since realized that I shouldn't hide how important my spirituality has been to my own development. In fact, I don't believe wholeness is possible without a spiritual dimension.

My own spiritual journey has coursed from Rome to Brazil, with many stops along the way. Born into an Italian family twenty-five miles north of Manhattan, we of course were Catholics. My grandmother and some of my uncles and aunts were steeped in Catholicism with frequent church attendance, rosaries, and other daily prayers. My own parents were Christmas and Easter Catholics while the rest of my large, extended family were mostly dutiful Catholics who usually attended Mass and didn't eat meat on Fridays. Perhaps out of closeness to my maternal grandmother and my attending Catholic school, I was among the most devout members of the family. I attended Mass frequently, said rosaries and prayers, and became an altar boy who served Masses, weddings, and funerals. I was very well versed in the Catechism; in fact, in both the seventh and eighth grades I won a gold medal in an interschool Catechism contest. More than once the thought of becoming a priest entered my mind.

Then came the inevitable hormonal surge bringing into painful awareness the attractiveness of the opposite sex. Somehow, as sexual interest filled the space of my being, the allure of priesthood and all things religious correspondingly diminished. Seeds of doubt were sown. How could anything so natural as sexual desire, sexual thoughts, self-pleasuring, or making out with a girlfriend be a mortal sin condemning our souls to eternal damnation?

By the time I completed four years in the US Air Force and entered college, doubt had become my creed. Agnosticism's famous prayer is "Oh God, if there is a God, save my soul, if I have a soul." From there to atheism wasn't too big a leap. Science was arriving with all the answers; why bother postulating the existence of a supreme being pulling the strings of creation and existence? I loved the smug certainty of believing religion was an opiate designed to numb and console its adherents who were simply unable to face the fact of eternal nonexistence.

This attitude lasted until my second year of graduate school. And then, along came lysergic acid diethylamide, more commonly known as LSD, and my smug certainty of atheism was shaken to its very core. I had already discovered I preferred marijuana to alcohol—no hangovers, no aggressiveness, only the munchies and a lot of "oh wows." And perhaps for the first time, a sense that sensations in my body—other than sexual sensations—could be pleasant. After some experimentation with LSD, mescaline, and psilocybin, I knew there was so much more to life than what scientific materialism and atheism had to offer. I had no idea what it was, but I knew the mystics, who have written throughout history, were on to something. My lenses of perception had opened just long enough, just wide enough, to get a glimpse of the mysterious. There would be no turning back.

It was eight years after my first encounter with LSD that my search for a spiritual path began in earnest. I was transitioning from working in a children's clinic to private practice when my friend Joseph Heller told me about a ten-day conference he'd just attended with a man named William Brugh Joy, MD. Brugh, as he was known, had been the medical director in a Los Angeles hospital when he became ill. Western medicine was unable to help him, but heeding a spiritual call did. He went off on a pilgrimage to India for some time and returned illness free. When he returned, he began teaching the subject "Living from the Heart Chakra or Living from Love." Joseph had attended Brugh's first conference in December 1975; I signed up for his next, January 1976. I had no idea what to expect other than it was about love. Money was tight and leaving my wife for ten days to attend a conference about love seemed a bit impetuous, but the call to attend was strong. I felt compelled to heed it.

I have very little memory of the first day of the conference, except that the food and accommodations were impressively first-class. However, the second day is indelibly etched in my heart and mind. I received a call from my wife, who said it was imperative she drive to the conference to talk to me. It was a two-and-a-half-hour drive each way, and I couldn't imagine what the urgency was. She arrived during our afternoon break with a somber, no-nonsense air. In a matter-of-fact way, she announced, "I want us to have an open marriage, and I've already begun."

My insides froze! I asked if she had anything else to tell me. She didn't, and I icily said goodbye. The conversation and her visit lasted less than two minutes. I did not remain frozen long as the rage and pain broke through the ice. I was livid and wanted to just smash things. Waves from rage to pain erupted.

In our group session that evening, Brugh and the group showered me with kindness and support. My own therapist and one of my dearest friends were members in the group. How fortunate to be in such a place at a time like this. I basked in their compassion. Yet the pain, grief, and rage were intense.

The next morning, after our group meditation, Brugh began his talk in the circle. What he said hit me almost as hard as the previous day's shocker. It was time to let go of the emotional reactivity, time to commit to working at the level of the heart. Enough emotionality! *What?* I could barely breathe. How was that even possible? I was still reeling, raging one moment, sobbing the next. Brugh said we had until our evening session to make a choice. Make the shift or go home. I was furious. Clearly, I was given an impossible assignment, and although he was addressing the whole group, I felt as if I was the only one in the room and he was talking only to me.

The rest of the morning and well into the afternoon were awful. I didn't know what to do. Never had I felt so much raw, primitive emotion. Even if there were no news of betrayal, the instruction to commit to the heart chakra would have been bizarre enough. Who does that? How? Slowly, I was preparing to leave the ranch, emotions still anything but settled.

And then (I know I'm straining my reader's credulity, but I swear to you it happened just as I am writing it), out of the blue, a most unusual and strange thing happened. My heart filled with love. Love! Not for anyone or anything in particular. I just felt love. What was happening to me? Where was this coming from? I was elated. Bewildered, but ecstatic! It wasn't as if the hurt and anger had been completely washed away. Both came in waves, but they were coming in a different context. I wasn't the victim of those emotions. I knew in my bones the love I was feeling was the presence of the divine. *From that moment on, my life was never the same.*

The next eight days of the conference were magical for me. One night as I was lying in bed preparing to sleep, I suddenly, eerily found myself on the ceiling looking down on my body. It was an immediate separation. Swish! I was on the ceiling (no substances whatsoever). My first thought was *I have to tell Brugh.* Then I became frightened and immediately slammed back into my body. I never had an experience quite like that before or since. Not like that.

All meals at the conference had a ritual element. At our dining table, all the seats were numbered one to fifteen. At the entrance to the dining hall was a basket with fifteen billiard balls. We were to reach in and pick one without any visual input, just grab a ball. From the day of my wife's visit until the day the conference ended, I picked billiard ball thirteen once every day. The odds of that occurring by chance are extremely unlikely!

Two weeks after the conference, I was taking a class back home in Santa Monica when the instructor walked in with billiard ball thirteen. A chill ran down my spine. Later that day I encountered the man with whom my wife had been sleeping. We had quite the conversation. Before returning from the conference, both my wife and I had reached the same conclusion. The marriage wasn't going to work; we deeply cared for each other, but the differences were irreconcilable, and it was best to amicably go our own ways, which was what we did.

To say my ten days with William Brugh Joy were among the most intense and phenomenal days of my life would be an understatement. I simply knew. There is a higher power! Clear, simple, and indisputable. If it were just the very low probability billiard ball selection, it would not have been so earthshaking. But for this young man with a severely traumatic childhood to suffer wrenching betrayal and find love in his heart and a clear, optimistic sense of future, obviously (to me) divine intervention was with me.

I "knew" there was a God, not a white-haired being in the sky sitting in judgment of me the way I had been taught but a superior intelligence, a superior force of love. My spiritual work, I have come to understand, is to align with this force. It's the work of a lifetime. I also received a knowing that my life was heading in a very positive direction, and in retrospect, it was indeed. My spiritual quest was now in full swing. For the first time in my life, I was frequently feeling peace in my heart and trust in my future.

After the conference with Brugh, I came across the teachings of the Unity Church, which I found appealing. I engaged them casually for a couple of years, when my ex-wife sent me a copy of *The Course in Miracles,*[2] and for the next three years, I was enchanted. The course was written by medical psychology professor Helen Schucman, who said she was merely a scribe channeling the voice of Jesus. *The Course in Miracles* includes working with an affirmation each day. There are 365 affirmations, such as "I'm never upset for the reason I think," "I am the light of the world," and "Forgiveness is my function as the light of the world." By working these thoughts throughout the day, I was cleansing my mind from swimming in the dark waters of my youth.

Further, *The Course's* views on love were similar to what I had learned from Brugh Joy. Specifically, love is a state of being, the radiance from which is to be bestowed upon my neighbor and myself. Reading *The Course* every day brought a new sense of tranquility into my life. At the time I was studying *The Course in Miracles*, I was living in Marin County, California. A couple of miles down the road in San Rafael was a center, including a bookstore, dedicated to the teachings of Da Free John.[3] I assume the majority of readers have never heard of Da Free John, but his writings are so powerful that the then-governor of California requested an audience with him. His books covered all of life: the body, nutrition, exercise, sex, and relationships all framed in a spiritual context. He has been called the greatest spiritual writer of all time. The wholistic nature of his theology appealed deeply. It was only a short time before I joined his community. As a member of Da Free John's community, the premise was that spiritual life was one's central focus. Having a guru may seem odd to most readers, but if we want to learn to play golf, it's natural to find a teacher or coach. No one would think that strange. If we want enlightenment, why would we not seek one who is enlightened? Da Free John never hesitated to remind his disciples that his enlightenment was of the highest stage, and the more we could focus our attention on him and his teachings, the better our chances of reaching a similar height of spiritual evolution. His books and his arguments were extremely compelling, even brilliant. But after a full year of active participation in what he called "Crazy Wisdom" teachings, I concluded that his writings contained wisdom, but his community practices were simply crazy.

In 1984, I left Da Free John and returned to potpourri spirituality. Then in 1991, Diane and I were introduced to the work of A. H. Almaas.[4] He also was a brilliant spiritual writer who combined a form of psychoanalysis—object relations theory—with Reichian bodywork and spirituality. Almaas's view was that the body/mind contractions needed to be released in order for us to evolve spiritually. He spoke my language. He called his work "Diamond Heart," which was a metaphor for human essence. Our essence is powerful, loving, strong, clear, soulful, and more.

These essence qualities require support as they begin to emerge in our early childhood; however, what happens most of the time is they are not supported. When they are not, we are left with a "hole" in our character, felt as a painful sense of deficiency far too intense to directly bear. In response to this early pain, we develop personality traits designed to mask the deficiency and allow us to function in our family and community. Essence is our approximation to the divine. At the beginning of our spiritual work, the stuff of ego and personality are huge, while the spark of essence is quite small in comparison. As we do our work acknowledging this painful sense of deficiency that underlies our tendencies, our essence grows; the stuff that's ego diminishes in comparison. Theoretically, I loved it. In practice, the method didn't seem to accomplish my expected results. In 1993 our Diamond Heart teacher in Seattle, Michael T., went to Brazil to give some talks on the Diamond Heart work. While there, some acquaintances invited him to attend a ceremony that involved drinking a mysterious tea generically known as ayahuasca. Later he said, "I was having a real experience of the concepts I had been teaching." What a statement! All of his teachings were about experiencing and integrating aspects of essence, but it was when he drank the tea that he really felt and knew without doubt those aspects he purported to teach. It was the beginning of the end of his Diamond Heart teaching career, and the Diamond Heart process for me.

A Sacred Substance

Back in the early 1960s, legitimate psychedelic research was occurring in the United States. When the drugs became popular with America's youth, Congress enacted the Controlled Substance Act, placing them all on their Schedule 1 list. This indicated they were considered dangerous and without medical value. Research came to a screeching halt. For decades the field was barren. Today, some fifty years later, there has been a renaissance of psychedelic research taking place in major universities such as Johns Hopkins. Further, there are dozens of schools, including the California Institute of Integral Studies, that offer a certificate in psychedelic-assisted therapies and research. Naropa, a Buddhist university in Boulder, Colorado began offering a course in MDMA-assisted psychotherapy in 2020 (Bloomberg News, January 17, 2021). MAPS (Multidisciplinary Association for Psychedelic

Studies) is a leading force committed to research, treatment, and education using psychedelics. Both the therapeutic and spiritual value of psychedelics are becoming recognized throughout the world.

After his first experience with ayahuasca, Michael invited a couple of the Brazilian *Mestres* to Seattle to distribute this mysterious tea. They belonged to a church, which had originated in Brazil and was known as the União do Vegetal (meaning Union of the Plants). From that first introduction in Seattle, different Mestres would come to Seattle each month to hold a "session" with the Vegetal (as the tea is called). As a student of Michael's, it wasn't long before I caught wind of the existence of this group. Diane and I immediately put our name on the waiting list.

October 1994 was probably the most stressful month of my adult life. After a beautiful and romantic three-week vacation in Italy, Diane and I were on our way home to Seattle when I was intercepted at Kennedy airport by my secretary informing me to call my family in New York. My mother had had a heart attack and was critical. I spent a week in New York with my family before returning to an extremely full private practice, workshops, and a new training in Vancouver. My mother died a week after that and back to New York I went, only to return to an even busier schedule. That was when I received the invitation. A space had opened and after a year's wait, I had the opportunity to drink the tea, known in the União do Vegetal (UDV) as Hoasca.

I arrived at the home of the assistant coordinator about thirty minutes prior to the scheduled beginning of the session and was immediately surprised at how warm the welcome was. Within an hour after drinking the tea, I knew I'd found what I'd long been seeking: such a profound feeling of peace and clarity. I could almost literally "see" the stress pouring out of my arms and hands.

Somewhere about two hours into the session, my mother appeared to me. It was as if she were there standing at my side. She looked young and beautiful! We didn't speak, just looked lovingly at each other. She had been gone about three weeks; we had had a very ambivalent relationship over the years. In an exchange of loving smiles, all that remained were peace and love. But what was most surprising occurred after the session. A friend who was sitting on the opposite side of the room came up to me and said, "Don, did you know your mother was here tonight?" Beyond stunned, I asked, "How do you know?" Without hesitating, he replied, "Because I saw her!" Imagine! The next day, to my surprise, I felt wonderful. No hangover, no fatigue. I had a full day of work, which flowed with ease and effectiveness. I didn't know anything about the UDV, but I knew I had found my church. This year I will be completing twenty-eight years as a participant.

Many people in the United States have drunk ayahuasca. Tours to Peru with shamans and ayahuasca experiences are easy to find on the internet. There are also many ayahuasca groups in cities throughout our country. In the past twenty years, I have had patients, friends, and acquaintances who have participated in ayahuasca rituals. However, there is a world of difference between experiencing this mysterious tea in an occasional ceremony with a visiting shaman versus participating as a member of the UDV with its structured ritual and vast body of teachings. The UDV is a spiritually rich and very connected way of life.

This spiritual path was officially created on July 22, 1961, by Jose Gabriel da Costa, known to his disciples as Mestre Gabriel. He was a simple yet extraordinary man who lived in the Amazon region of Brazil with his wife and children. After drinking ayahuasca for the first time, he realized his mission was to create the UDV with the intention of helping to bring peace on earth. Stories about him from those who knew him well, including his siblings, portray a man with extraordinary physical prowess. As a child, he could ride a horse backward while standing on his feet. With little formal training in the art of capoeira, he could engage and match capoeira masters. His psychic ability was equally extraordinary. I once asked one of his first disciples how he came to accept Mestre Gabriel as a genuine spiritual teacher. His response was "When he demonstrated he could enter into another's mind and know what the other person was thinking." My skeptical response was "How did you know he was actually doing that?"

Without hesitating, he responded, "Because one time he took me with him and allowed me to read a person's thoughts. His kindness, humility, and generosity are revealed in the following story. Mestre Gabriel once had a neighbor who was critical of him and his work. This neighbor was poor and could barely put enough food on her table. So every week, Gabriel would have a basket of food delivered to her door; he made sure she had no idea where the food was coming from. After his death, the food stopped being delivered and the neighbor sought to discover why it no longer came. That was when she discovered it was Gabriel who had been sending it to her.

By May 1999, over 10,000 people were following the path of the UDV, including several hundred in the United States. It was that month the federal government's Drug Enforcement Agency raided the office of Jeffrey Bronfman, who at the time was responsible for the UDV in the US. For several months, the government held the threat of prosecution over us while we attempted to convince them we were a bona fide religion practicing within our rights under the US Constitution. After several months of not making any progress with persuasion, the UDV in the US, led by Mr. Bronfman, filed suit in the Federal District Court in Albuquerque. David challenged Goliath in what appeared to the outsider to be a quixotic attempt to score an impossible victory. There were approximately three hundred of us in the US at that time, and although we had resources, compared to the government of the United States, we were grossly mismatched.

The court battles continued for five years. Throughout this time, each of our groups—in Seattle, Santa Fe, Norwood, Colorado, Dallas, and San Francisco—continued our sessions drinking water rather than our Hoasca tea. We drank water as an expression of our faith that given the righteousness and justice of our cause, we would prevail. Prevail we did! We won in four different court rooms: the Federal District Court in Albuquerque, the Tenth

Circuit Court of Appeals in Denver, the Tenth Circuit Court en banc (all thirteen members present), and finally, in a unanimous decision, the United States Supreme Court. David defeated Goliath, and the Beneficent Spiritist Center União do Vegetal was legally confirmed in the United States of America.

The word *religion* means to "reconnect." What does that really mean? We have already spoken about connection to body, to self, to each other, to community, and to nature. Religion adds connection to source. It was 1976 when I had my first spiritual awakening. I felt the presence of the existence of a superior power, a superior intelligence, in my life. This recognition was my first step, and remembering this presence in a deep feeling way is an ongoing process in my spiritual growth. Without this recognition, we experience ourselves as separate creatures left to our own devices in denial of a fundamental truth: we are connected to something beyond ourselves. Throughout every culture studied by anthropologists, human beings have had stories that connected them to the cosmos. However simplistic many of those stories were, they nevertheless provided people with a sense of belonging to something beyond their own individuality. They were linked to the cosmos. They had a place, and their place fit well into the whole of creation. The teachings and stories of the UDV help us to find our place in the cosmos.

Drinking our sacred tea, Hoasca, is the resource we have in the UDV to help us feel the presence of the divine. Nature has provided tools for us to learn to open toward divinity. We drink this tea for the purpose of mental concentration, which is the common denominator of meditation, prayer, and the focus involved in bringing intentions to fruition.

There is a spark of the divine in each and every one of us. Growing that spark is our spiritual work; it includes discovering and transforming all within us that blocks the growth of this divine spark. I'm speaking of things like vanity, envy, pride, jealousy, resentment, anger, beliefs of our inadequacy, shame, guilt, fear, being judgmental, feelings of inferiority, and feelings of superiority.

Further, the work is not just about finding and letting go of negativity, addictions, and vices. It's also about developing virtues. Patience, equilibrium, tranquility, integrity, transparency, intellectual development, humility, fidelity, honesty (especially about ourselves), practicing goodness, and so many more are virtues important to spiritual development. It takes a lifelong commitment to do this work. It requires practice, patience, and discernment to do spiritual work.

Spiritual work is just that—work. It requires the development of a strong center and high degree of self-acceptance in order to examine the depths of our consciousness and not flinch at what we discover. It's hard because it requires a willingness to face and bring to light all those dark recesses of our being. Our culture doesn't support this; transformation is not one of our world's primary values. We can consider this yet another cultural wounding. It is also hard because it requires facing our beauty, our power, our capacity, our light, and our goodness. These can be as challenging to embrace as our darkness.

As we have seen, we can trace most of our challenges to woundings and insufficient development of three dimensions of being: responsibility, identity, and connection. Starting with responsibility, we learn that it is impossible to grow spiritually from the place of victimhood. Taking responsibility for how we respond, for how we deal with what we are given, and for how we contribute to what we receive is a powerful teaching.

Concerning identity, we come to understand that we are spirits in a process of evolution. In my comprehension, if we are spirits inhabiting a body, then any rigid self-construct is an imposed limitation on our potential for manifestation. So much human suffering stems from the attempt to fit into a preconceived identity box that is suffocating. Most of us are so much more than we take ourselves to be.

The third dimension is connection, the feeling sense of being linked to ourselves, our depths, and our bodies. It involves connection to an intimate other, one that's real, honest, and transparent;

connection to family and friends, a sense of community; connection to nature; and connection to the cosmos. We are part of the whole. It's one thing to know that as an abstract concept; it's another to have a felt-sense. This is the whole to which we belong.

In her beautiful book *Good Chemistry: The Science of Connection from Soul to Psychedelics*,[5] Julie Holland, MD, postulates that loneliness or absence of sufficient nourishing connection underlies some of our most intractable problems. So much suffering from addictions, depression, anxiety, relationship distress, even chronic disease, has its roots in the lack of strong, positive connections. The great pandemic of our time—worse than COVID 19, because it determines our ability to deal effectively with the virus—is our massive disconnection and the bone-chilling loneliness that ensues. This pandemic of loneliness with all its virulent variations underlies our most serious social, behavioral, and health challenges. This entire book describes just how this occurs.

There is much suffering in the world, and there is so much goodness in the world. So much beauty! So many exquisite and breathtaking vistas in nature. So many good, wonderful, beautiful, kind, and caring people. So many pockets of light! So much good work being done to help those in need. So many scientific discoveries to help us stay healthy and to live comfortably. So many opportunities to heal and grow. How do we hold all of this? All of the ugliness and all of the beauty?

We continue to open our hearts, knowing our hearts can hold both.

Conclusion

We've traveled a long way together. We understand now that wounds are ubiquitous, both familial and cultural. This understanding can encourage us all to embark on what I have termed an adventure of a lifetime, a process of healing those wounds. It's a process of becoming whole, integrated, and discovering and expressing our true, essential nature, which is both coherent and fluid. With support, comprehension, practices and sometimes the medicines of nature, we are capable of finding our place on this earth, our inherent belonging, value, strength, heart-felt expression, vulnerability, our capacity for connection, intimacy, love and meaning, our sense of responsibility, authorship for our lives, and a fuller, richer sense of self.

Notes

1. Smith, Huston, *Why Religion Matters*, Harper Collins, 2001, 23–41.
2. Schucman, Helen, *A Course in Miracles, Foundation for Inner Peace*, 1975.
3. Da Free John has written over thirty books. Many are available on Amazon.
4. Almaas, A. H., *Essence: The Diamond Heart Approach to Inner Realization*, Samuel Weiser Inc., 1986.
5. Holland, Julie, *Good Chemistry: The Science of Connection From Soul to Psychedelics*, Harper Collins, 2020

Bibliography

Childre, Doc and Cryer Bruce. *From Chaos to Coherence*. Boulder Creek, Ca: Planetary, 2004.

Conrad, Emilie. *Life on Land: The Story of Continuum: The World-Renowned Self-Discovery and Movement Method*. Berkeley: North Atlantic Books, 2007.

Ecker Bruce and Hulley Laurel. *Depth Oriented Brief Therapy*. San Francisco: Jossey-Bass, 1996.

Everly, George and Lating, Jeffrey. *A Clinical Guide to the Treatment of the Human Stress Response*. New York: Kluwer Academic/Plenum Publishers, 2002.

Fogel, Alan. *The Psychophysiology of Self Awareness: Rediscovering the Lost Art of Body Sense*. New York: W. W. Norton, 2009.

Fosha, Diana. *The Transforming Power of Affect*. New York: Basic Books, 2002.

Fredrickson, Barbara. *Love 2.0: Creating Happiness and Health in Moments of Connection*. New York: Plume, 2013.

Gilligan, Stephen. *The Courage to Love: Principles and Practices of Self-Relations Psychotherapy*. New York: W.W. Norton, 1997.

Hanna, Thomas. *The Body of Life*. New York, Alfred A Knopf, Inc. 1979.

Hanna, Thomas. *Somatics*. Cambridge: Perseus Books, 1988.

Hanson, Rick. *Buddha's Brain. Oakland, Ca: New Harbinger Publications, 2009.*

Hanson, Rick. *Hardwiring Happiness*. New York: Harmony Books, 2013.

Heller, Joseph. *Bodywise: Regaining Your Natural Flexibility and Vitality for Maximum Well-Being*. Los Angeles: Jeremy P. Tarcher, Inc. 1986.

Ho, Mae-Wan. *The Rainbow and the Worm: The Physics of Organisms*. River Edge, N.J.: World Scientific Publishing, 1998.

Ho, Mae-Wan. *Living Rainbow H2O*. Hackensack, N.J.: World Scientific Publishing, 2012.

Holdrege, Craig, ed. *The Dynamic Heart and Circulation*. Fair Oaks, Ca.: The Association of Waldorf Schools of North America, 2002

Holland, Julie. *Good Chemistry: The Science of Connection from Soul to Psychedelics*, New York, Harper Collins, 2020.

Johnson, Susan. *The Practice of Emotionally Focused Marital Therapy: Creating Connection*. Philadelphia: Brunner/Mazel, Inc., 1996.

Kaufman, Gershen. *Shame: The Power of Caring*. Cambridge: Schenkman Books, 1980.

Kaufman, Gershen. *The Psychology of Shame: Theory and Treatment of Shame Based Syndromes*. New York: Springer Publishing Co., 1996.

Koob, Andrew. *The Root of Thought: Unlocking Glia, the Brain Cell That Will Help Us Sharpen Our Wits, Heal Injury, and Treat Brain Disease*. Upper Saddle River, New Jersey: Pearson Education Inc. 2009.

Levine, Peter. *Waking the Tiger*. Berkeley: North Atlantic Books, 1997.

Levine, Peter. *In An Unspoken Voice: How the Body Releases Trauma and Restores Goodness*. Berkeley: North Atlantic Books, 2010.

Levoy, Gregg. *Callings: Finding and Following an Authentic Life*. New York: Three Rivers Press, 1997.

Loehr, Jim and Schwartz, Tony. *The Power of Full Engagement*. New York: Simon and Schuster, 2003.

McEwen, Bruce. *The End of Stress As We Know It*. Washington, D. C: Joseph Henry Press, 2002.

Nathanson, Donald. *Shame and Pride: Affect, Sex, and the Birth of the Self*. New York: W. W. Norton, 1992.

Ornish Dean. *Love and Survival: The Scientific Basis for the Healing Power of Intimacy*. New York: Harper Collins, 1998.

Pearsall, Paul. *The Heart's Code*. New York: Broadway Books, 1998.

Pert, Candace. *The Molecules of Emotion.* New York: Scribner, 1997.

Pollack, Gerald. *The Fourth Phase of Water.* Seattle: Ebner and Sons Publishers, 2013.

Porges, Stephen. *The Polyvagal Theory: Neurophysiological Foundations of Emotions, Attachment, Communication and Self-Regulation.* New York: W. W. Norton. 2011.

Reich, Wilhelm. *The Function of the Orgasm.* Meridian Books, 1927.

Reich, Wilhelm. *Selected Writings.* New York: Farrar, Straus and Giroux, 1951.

Richo, David. *How To Be An Adult in Relationships.* Boston: Shambhala Publications, 2002.

Rolf, Ida P. *Rolfing: The Integration of Human Structures.* New York: Harper and Row, 1977.

Schore, Allan N. *Affect Regulation and the Origin of the Self.* Hillsdale: Lawrence Erlbaum Associates, 1994.

Schultz, Louis and Feitis, Rosemary. *The Endless Web: Fascial anatomy and physical reality. Berkeley: North Atlantic Books, 1996.*

Siegel, Dan. *The Developing Mind: Toward a Neurobiology of Interpersonal Relation.* New York: The Guilford Press, 1999.

Siegel, Dan. *The Mindful Brain.* New York: W. W. Norton and Company, 2007.

Solomon, Marion F. and Siegel, Daniel J. ed. *Healing Trauma*. New York: W. W. Norton, 2003.

Schwenk, Theodor. *Sensitive Chaos: The Creation of Flowing Forms in Water and Air*. London: Rudolph Steiner Press, 1965.

Stone, Hal and Stone, Sidra. *Embracing Our Selves*. Marina del Rey, Ca: Devorss & Co., 1985.

Stone, Hal and Stone, Sidra. *Partnering: A New Kind of Relationship: How to Love Each Other Without Losing Yourselves*. Novato, Ca: New World Library, 2000.

Stone, Hal and Stone, Sidra. *The Fireside Chats with Hal and Sidra Stone*. Albion, Ca: Delos, Inc. 2011.

Todd, Mabel Elsworth. *The Thinking Body*. Brooklyn, N.Y: Dance Horizons, 1972.

Van Der Kolk, Bessel. *The Body Keeps the Score*. New York: The Penguin Group, 2014.

Van Der Kolk, Bessel, McFarlane, Alexander and Weisaeth, L. *Traumatic Stress: The effects of overwhelming experience on mind, body and society*. New York: The Guilford Press, 1996.

Wirth, Fredrick. *Prenatal Parenting*. New York: Harper Collins, 2001.

For information about our work or to set up lectures, workshops or in-person or telephone appointments, please visit **www.pathsofconnection.com** or email me at **don@st-jon.com**